# Battle with the Dark Side

## My Journey from
## Teacher to Exorcist

**Laura Van Tyne**

LIGHT STREAM
FOUNDATION

Battle with the Dark Side: My Journey from Teacher to Exorcist
Published by Light Stream Foundation
Oregon City, Oregon, U.S.A.

VAN TYNE, LAURA, Author
BATTLE WITH THE DARK SIDE
LAURA VAN TYNE

Library of Congress Control Number: 2024916002

ISBN: 979-8-9900334-5-0, 979-8-9900334-8-1 (paperback)
ISBN: 979-8-9900334-6-7, 979-8-9900334-9-8 (hardcover)
ISBN: 979-8-9900334-7-4 (digital)

**BODY, MIND & SPIRIT** / Unexplained Phenomena
**FAMILY & RELATIONSHIPS** / Parenting / Single Parent
**BIOGRAPHY & AUTOBIOGRAPHY** / Social Scientists & Psychologists
**EDUCATION** / Non-Formal Education

Book Design, Cover Design and E-book formatting:
Amit Dey (amitdey2528@gmail.com)
Publishing Management: Susie Schaefer (finishthebookpublishing.com)

QUANTITY PURCHASES: Schools, companies, professional groups, clubs, and other organizations may qualify for special terms when ordering quantities of this title.
For information, email lightstreamfdn@proton.me

# DEDICATION

This book is dedicated to parents of psychic children. Raising children has never been more challenging, and adding the psychic ingredient makes everything even more complicated.

It is a daunting task to protect your child from the normal seen world-- that world that we can see, hear, touch, taste. What happens when your child starts communicating with ghosts and other entities in another dimension? The unseen world? How do you know that what is communicating with your child is in your child's best interest? How do you keep them safe? How do we discern the good guys from the bad? In the physical realms, we know that we don't send our five-year-olds to the park by themselves to buy ice cream. Why would it be ok to let your child talk to a stranger from another realm without your permission or knowledge?

In addition to parents of psychic children, this book is dedicated to those struggling to understand their psychic abilities, to those trying to understand the impacts of the energies in these other dimensions that cross over into our mortal lives, and to those who are learning how to keep our souls strong and healthy.

teach·er

/ˈtēCHər/

*noun*

One who or that which teaches or instructs; an instructor; also figurative; spec. one whose function is to give instruction, esp. in a school.

ex·or·cist

/ˈekˌsôrˌsəst,ˈeksərˌsəst/

*noun*

1. a person who <u>expels</u> or attempts to <u>expel</u> a supposed evil spirit from a person or place by adjuration.

2. A person who gets rid of something troublesome, menacing, or oppressive.

# TABLE OF CONTENTS

# PROLOGUE

To my family, while we have not had a traditional life, I will always work to move mountains for us. My love for you is eternal. We made it through these dark times.

My ex-husband worked endlessly supporting our family throughout this nightmarish situation into which we were thrown. Finding balance and normalcy was never easy. And thank you for validating me to write this story. I appreciate your support.

Trying to protect our children from the nefarious, unseen, energetic world under the assumption of living a normal life was difficult, but we made it! We lived a secret life for many years. Today, times are different as people are more open to this type of information, which is what will save humanity. We need to remember that knowledge is power.

# INTRODUCTION

I was a schoolteacher with three girls in elementary school. My husband was a businessman. We were the typical middle-class southern California family juggling hectic but rewarding schedules of school, work, soccer practice, and birthday parties. Then, one day, I was tossed into the deep end of the paranormal pool. I think it is safe to say that I was thrown in with a pair of cement shoes. Our home became a ghost super-highway, and it wasn't just ghosts. It included other beings that I never knew existed. We were now living a life that eerily mirrored a Hollywood horror movie. The stuff nightmares are made of, only these nightmares were our reality.

It all started with my daughter, who was six years old at the time. It was as if a psychic switch suddenly flipped into the on position, and our lives were sent into motion into a world that resembled Earth but not reality. Our beautiful, secure family would be shaken to its core for almost a decade. My cute little girl could see through walls and doors in multiple dimensions.

At the time, I had no idea that this was even possible. I had no idea how to Google some of these actions she was doing before the internet became what it is today. I lacked the vocabulary. I couldn't even form a logical question. For example, one night, while cooking dinner, I asked my daughter what was on my bed. She paused. She closed her eyes and said a $20 bill. I was stunned at her accuracy.

She could also see and talk to all sorts of entities and beings my husband and I were not privy to. As parents, we felt blind and deaf. We felt vulnerable. We WERE vulnerable. It is much easier to protect your child from the seen elements. Our home was being invaded, and we had no idea what to do about our new visitors. We have all heard stories about kids talking to imaginary friends, but maybe, just maybe, those friends aren't so imaginary.

In our case, these beings were not at all friendly. They sought to hurt my daughter and me on many levels, both physically, mentally, and psychically. I didn't understand why. My family may never know all the myriad of reasons why we had to endure the horror over those long years.

In an instant, the paranormal took over our lives.

The obvious speculation as to why would lead me to conclude that this book would not have been possible had my family not experienced this paranormal activity. Secondly, I soon realized that they were after me, and these dark beings were using my daughter as bait.

But why?

I was beyond terrified. Every day, I had to push back this cloak of paralyzing fear and move forward. I was not going to let them win. If they were to win, it would have meant I would lose my family, and that was never, ever an option.

I was also determined not to repeat what my parents had done to me: discourage a phenomenon they didn't understand by no fault of their own. While my daughter's psychic ability grew, mine returned.

Growing up in a small southwestern Michigan town, my parents discouraged my ability. Still, during these threats and assaults on my little girl, my abilities came rushing back at a pace so strong that I wasn't even able to share it with my closest friends for fear of being ostracized. I was barely able to understand the shift myself. How could I possibly explain it to those closest to me?

Eventually, I had to leave my job as a teacher to learn to protect my family. This was my new job—a job I never could have imagined. It ended up being more than a job. It became my mission. I was in the midst of a spiritual war that I never knew was possible or existed. I had much to learn, and the information was hard to find. And this is the reason why I am here today.

Growing up, my abilities eventually faded away, and life went on. However, as my daughter's abilities grew, mine came back. Based on my upbringing, I knew what NOT to do. I also knew I needed help. My daughter's abilities were way different than what I had as a kid. I needed to learn, to study, to find answers.

The only power I had to rely upon was my intuition. Along the way, I learned about the power of intuition: how to develop it, how to trust the gut reaction we all have, and, most importantly, how not to deny myself that inner truth.

Many times, I felt like a failure as a parent because I didn't know how to protect and help her. As much as I wanted to cry, I couldn't. I couldn't show my fear to my family. The isolation and loneliness were excruciating. No one really knew the depths of the gravity of this crazy situation. I couldn't cry myself to sleep because I couldn't sleep.

If I were to fall asleep, what would they do to my little girl?

It wasn't unusual for cabinet doors to fling open—for a random dish to fly off the table and shatter. One evening, our family went to an art exhibit on Middle Eastern Art; when we arrived home, I opened the front door, and we all saw the 4 x 5-foot acrylic painting in the living room stretch from the inside out as if there was a finger pushing it out about 4 inches. We took it off the wall, cut it up, and burned it.

Hiring a babysitter to come over so my husband and I could attend a nice dinner was out of the question. A weekend getaway with just the two of us was not an option. This was because it wasn't just ghosts that took up residence in our home.

If that wasn't bad enough, one night, I heard this tiny pair of feet racing down the hallway, and my precious little girl leaped into bed with us. I swear she must have jumped 10 feet. She then held me tight and told me in a very soft whisper, "Mom, I heard the bad shadow men talking in my room. I heard them say that we are too powerful, and they want to take my soul so that it crushes you. What does it mean to take my soul? Why do they want to hurt you? Mommy, I'm scared."

Then she started to cry. I held her as tightly as I could while holding back my own tears of fear. As her protector and mother, I could not let her know how terrified I was.

To make matters worse, at that time, I couldn't SEE what I was supposed to protect her FROM. After that night forward and for the many, many months that followed, I slept in my daughter's bed as I prayed for help and guidance. I held back my own tears for fear that she would discover how bad this situation was.

I needed to be strong, and I was barely surviving. I couldn't fully confide in my husband because he needed to be able to focus at work and not be distracted.

The paranormal activity continued on and on, exhausting us all and constantly testing our will and fortitude. This was never something we asked for; it didn't come about because one of us was 'dabbling' in something we shouldn't have been doing. Finding answers and solutions became my priority.

In my quest to find spiritual help to protect my family from the unseen world, I consulted with hundreds of religious, spiritual, and psychic practitioners. I learned a lot from every single one of them. I had to figure this out. I had to protect my family.

That is why I chose to write this book.

I have many stories to share about what happened to our family. This book allows me to share what I know to be true about the spiritual influences that affect our lives.

Along this wild, windy journey, I came to understand that we are all spiritual beings. A higher realization is that not all spiritual beings play for the same team. Surprisingly, not all humans accurately represent their physical appearance.

The physical bodies we are born with are a cloak for what lies beneath the surface of emotion, brain waves, intuition, and the love that pulses in and out of us. In everything we do, in every encounter we make, there are lessons to be learned. This is the beauty of Karma, though we may not know or recognize it at the time.

The first section of this book features a variety of true ghost stories. Each one is unique and offers lessons and examples about ghost energies, how they impact us, and the importance of remembering that a ghost is simply a former human without a shell.

Ghosts all need our help to return Home to the higher realms.

# Section 1

·····◆·····

# PARANORMAL PERILS

# LIVING INSIDE A HORROR MOVIE

**"I see dead people."**

This is the line from *The Sixth Sense*, starring Bruce Willis and Haley Joel Osment. I didn't want to watch this movie. I put off watching it for a long time. The first time I saw that movie was in 2012, yet the thriller premiered in 1999.

All I could think about was, "Wow. That boy is so lucky. He only sees one or two dead people at a time."

This was the beginning of a long journey down the paranormal rabbit hole, with the constant questions in the back of my mind: "Am I going crazy?" "Is this real?" We were living inside our own thriller movie, and the end credits never rolled across the screen.

What happens when your child sees dead people and other paranormal activity that most people do not even know exists or refuse to believe exists? How do you stay 'normal'? How do you get help? How do you know it is the 'right' help?

That help eluded me for what seemed like an eternity. This is how it all began.

In retrospect, the paranormal hauntings started slow, but only because I didn't know what my daughter was going through. She didn't talk about it. She thought what she was hearing was normal, and everyone else could hear these hauntings, too.

She was about six years old when she started hearing noises, but nothing was there. At first, she said nothing because she assumed the rest of our family could hear those footsteps around the house. I remembered her asking me if I could hear "that noise."

"Hear what?" I asked.

And that was the end of our conversation. Little did I know what was to come in the near future.

When my dad died, it was the sucker punch of a lifetime. In many ways, he was 'my person'. We had always connected on many levels; we could finish each other's thoughts. Philosophically, we were aligned. He was always full of great advice on so many topics.

He and my stepmom traveled to southern California one summer just so they could build their granddaughters a 'playhouse' in the backyard. This 8X10 structure sported dual pane windows insulation and even had its own air conditioning unit.

The grief I experienced at losing him still pops up every now and then.

The prior year, both of my husband's parents died. They were elderly and in poor health, yet they lived full lives, and I grew to love them as much as my parents. We knew their end time was near.

My husband and I took care of both of them. I would take them to their doctor appointments and help with cleaning and groceries. My husband would stay the night with them to make sure they were safe. It was exhausting. We had three kids under the age of five and two over the age of 75.

I still love them dearly to this day, and when they died within six months of each other, I told myself it was a blessing. They succumbed due to the deterioration of their failing health.

Our children missed their grandparents. They lived close to us, and in that one year, all of our family traditions changed—all of those holiday events now needed to be at a different location. Grandma and Grandpa's house was no more. My children would never again get birthday and holiday cards filled with stickers and other fun items from them in the mail. My husband and I would never be able to watch our girls rip open these cards and squeal in delight as they got to spread those little treasures out all over our dining room table.

## The Year of Firsts

When a loved one dies, all those family traditions die with them. All those traditions that ground us and reconnect us are gone. Those celebrations with family and friends coming together are what make those eternal memories that shape us and guide us. Our family needed to move forward to create new traditions.

I was talking to my dad about this and how, this past Halloween, the girls realized they didn't get cards with Halloween stickers in the mail from Grandpa George and Grandma Millie. Thanksgiving was coming up, and there would be not one but two empty seats at our table this year.

The next day, I got a call from my dad. I didn't even say hello before he blurted out --

"I found plane tickets from Chicago to Las Vegas for $39 round trip and hotel rooms for $29 (at this new and fancy hotel). How about you all drive to Las Vegas and meet us there for Thanksgiving?"

Recalling this conversation makes me want to laugh and cry.

Here is my dad, whom the day before I was crying to about how certain family traditions have changed and how our girls don't have much family close by. He takes this as an opportunity to delve into his newest passion since his recent retirement: How cheap can my wife and I travel around the world? It was like a game for him, and he loved every minute of it.

I immediately said yes and told our family we were about to have an adventure for Thanksgiving.

We were all so excited as we packed up the van for our trip to Las Vegas. The drive was fun. We were all singing and chatting in the car, with the constant drone of "Are we there yet?" coming from various back seats. However, as we entered this gritty city, I felt an overwhelming pang of sadness that I couldn't explain. It's incredible how our emotional states can vacillate so quickly and unexpectedly.

As we got closer to the hotel, I called my dad so he and my stepmom could meet us at the front of the hotel where they were staying. I gave my dad a huge hug and felt something was horribly wrong, but I could not figure out what it was.

I shrugged off the prickly feeling, thinking it was just my own strange vibe. Was that just me, or did Dad feel it, too?

When my dad spotted his treasured granddaughters, he was like a kid in a candy shop. He may have been more excited about this trip than our girls if that was possible. It turned out this hotel had a bowling alley, and my dad couldn't wait to take his granddaughters bowling. This struck me as hysterical because I don't think my dad ever bowled a day in his life.

As he took off with his three granddaughters, all holding hands and literally bouncing down the hallway to get to the elevator, they eventually disappeared. At this moment, I looked at my stepmom and asked,

"What's wrong with my dad," I asked.

"What do you mean," she asked. "He's fine and is having the time of his life right now."

And that is when I blurted out, "He's going to die soon. Something is really, really wrong. You have to get him to a doctor when you get back. Promise me."

She tried to reassure me, "His back has been hurting, but he's been doing a lot of stuff around the house. He doesn't need to go to the doctor for a simple backache."

I told her I was sorry I had alarmed her and had no idea where that came from. But I knew...

Looking back, I handled myself all wrong. I shouldn't have blurted this information out to my stepmom. It wasn't fair to her. I did not know or understand how I got this 'message' or prediction of his upcoming death. I had a knee-jerk reaction to this intuitive thought. Or was it an intuitive thought?

When I hugged him, I felt it; I felt an unexplainable vibration, and I somehow saw it. How was it that I knew he was ill and going to die? There were no precursors, no indications he was sick.

All I knew was that we were always exceptionally close. We could finish each other's sentences and think the same thoughts. He was a teacher, and I became a teacher because of him. He advocated for those in need, and I followed in his footsteps.

I got the call ten days after our Las Vegas visit. "Your dad has been admitted to the hospital, and they are transferring him to a larger regional hospital. His backache got so bad I had to take him to the emergency room last night. They have done blood work, and they think he has pancreatic cancer. But nothing is definite yet."

But I knew. To this day, those words echo in my head.

I now realize what I saw in Vegas was that an etheric rigor mortis had set in, and that is why he appeared 'grey' to me when I saw him. But I didn't understand that at the time.

Also, one of my biggest regrets was that I should have never disclosed that information to my stepmom. It only instilled the fear that this was a death sentence.

My dad died six weeks later, and our new Thanksgiving tradition died with him.

It was shortly after his death that our daughter started hearing footsteps and breathing noises in our house. I just never put the two together. She had been hearing these noises for almost a year and never really said anything about it.

One night, I was lying in bed with our daughter, reading her a bedtime story. That's when my dad, my deceased dad, put his hand on her arm, and she could feel him. She couldn't see him, but she could feel him and identify him. I asked her how she knew it was her Grandpa Russ.

Her simple reply was, "Because it *feels* like him. And his breaths sound like his breaths."

The next afternoon, my little girl was doing her homework at the dining room table when she suddenly started laughing. She said Grandpa Russ was here, and he was making faces at her. She could see him now, and she was excited about that.

I just stood there. I was dumbfounded. What did this mean? I just assumed my dad went to Heaven. If that's the case, how is it that he is here? In my dining room? Can deceased loved ones come back here for vacation? I had no idea what to think when, unexpectedly, my dad, who was now a ghost, delivered an ominous message to me through my daughter.

"Grandpa Russ has a message for you. He says, '*I'm here to protect you.*' Then she looked at me confused and continued, "Grandpa says he must couch his messages to you, and you have to read between the lines."

"What does that mean? Couches are for sitting on, and when you read, there is just blank paper between the lines. What's to read there? I don't get this," said my very literal and innocent six-year-old.

The "spidey" senses that would eventually become stronger in me started to grow in the pit of my stomach. To my harsh realization, I thought, "Good grief, this child is spunky and doesn't miss a beat!"

This began a new journey as we unknowingly entered another dimension, an alternate realm without experience. My dad told me, "What I could see and do could be seen in many dimensions. A lot of darkness will come your way." I felt like he was trying to warn us.

This left me quite unnerved. I will also admit I didn't fully comprehend that message for a long time.

I realized that during this past year, I was unaware that my dad was 'living' with us. Sometimes, I could sense his presence, and that was comforting. I really did miss him. He was the only family that I felt close to growing up. I thought he was checking in on us, not becoming our daughter's de facto bodyguard.

Did this mean that he had chosen to stay with us? Could he cross over and come back? How did this work? Was he even supposed to be here? I had so many questions that needed answers.

## The Message

I asked my little translator to ask Grandpa what he meant by 'lots of bad things.'

She replied, "Grandpa says that there are many bad things in the other world, and he is staying here to protect you and me from them."

Again, I asked, "What bad things, and what do I need to know?"

All he would tell her (knowing him, he probably did not want to scare her too much) was that many evil beings would want to come after us. I sensed he was staying to protect her and us. Then I realized he didn't want to go into more detail to avoid scaring my daughter.

As the days, weeks, and months continued, we understood he was with her 24/7. He would go to school with her, go to soccer and karate with her, and stand by her bed at night, guarding her.

In the meantime, we had many conversations with him. Conversations that I thought we would never have the opportunity to have again. He would play games and sing to her.

One day in class, a boy was teasing her, so my dad grabbed the boy's ankle.

The boy yelled, 'Hey, who did that?' Boy, did she get a kick out of that. She knew that was her grandpa sticking up for her.

This was the first of many protective encounters my ghost dad would provide. Little did I know what was to come. My anticipation heightened.

Ultimately, I knew that I could not allow my ghost dad to be her protector and help my daughter, no matter how well-intentioned. The protection I knew I needed and sought from unidentified beings must come from another source. I would have to learn how to protect her and my family, but from *what?* What was so threatening?

To say I was dumbfounded would have been a glorious understatement. My learning curve would have to grow fast, and I was clueless about what I needed to know.

# SHE ZAPPED HIM WITH
# A BLUE LIGHT


"**M**o-oooom! Mom-Mom-Mom! Guess what?" she shrieked as she ran out of her bedroom to find me.

I stood there, frozen, wondering what would pop out of my child's mouth this time. The one factor I did know was that when she said the word "mom," and it contained more than one syllable, something unbelievably weird and unnerving was about to happen. I was in a hurry, trying to make breakfast and lunches for our daughters and get them to school. I didn't have time for this, but I had to make the time. I knew it would be important.

"Yes, hon, what's up?" I replied, still making sandwiches.

"Mom! Guess what? Guess what happened! I was lying in bed, about to get up and get dressed, when this bad ghost-spirit-man came into my room! He told me he wanted MY body, and I told him, "No way." And he tried to get inside my body right here." She said, pushing her long, curly blonde hair out of her face and pointing to her solar plexus.

I dropped the knife that was in my hand, and my jaw hit the floor. I wanted to scream, "What? Are you ok?" But I didn't. I had to appear at least to remain cool, calm, and collected.

"And he got halfway in! Feet first! And then I said "NO," and I zapped him with my hands like this! Then guess what? This electric blue light shot out of my hands. It was so cool!" She then pushes her arms and hands out, her palms facing out, showing me how she zapped him.

"And then I zapped him again and again and again! I zapped him! I zapped him, Mom! And he left!" Our spunky six-year-old walked off to get dressed for school and was so proud of herself.

Welcome to our new normal. Where every day was different, and I could never predict what that *different* would be. My imagination was, well, quite frankly, completely exhausted and not that good.

After recovering from my initial shock, I regained my composure, trying to prove to myself that I was in control of this situation, but I knew I wasn't. I realized that this was some type of attempted possession. She was so proud of herself yet so oblivious to the danger of the entire situation. Somehow, my vibrant little six-year-old managed to defend herself against some unseen malevolent force and avoid possession.

I summoned a relaxed smile on my face. I had to pretend that this was normal and somehow ok. I didn't want her to know what happened here. I didn't want to give her my fear.

If I instilled fear and doubt in her, this could be really dangerous. It might erode her confidence and natural and ever-expanding psychic abilities, many of which I had difficulty understanding. The world is flooded with many parenting books, but there is no book on what we were experiencing. This new normal was painfully lonely and terrifying on the good days.

"That's great. Let's keep this between us, ok? Did you brush your hair and teeth yet? We can't be late for school. . . again." As I said this to her, my knees were literally shaking. I had to work hard to manage a steady voice. Children need to know that their parents are in control and that they are there for their children no matter what. Fifteen minutes later, I was a typical mom again, dropping off my kids at the front of the school.

That was one of many days I will never forget. I felt like we dodged a bullet. Wait, we *did* dodge a bullet. On my way home, I wondered how many other children and adults had experienced an attempted possession or had something like this happen to them. How many people have not known innately what to do or had parents or someone who they could tell or share what happened to them? Is this what multiple personalities are about? How common is this? What would have happened had my daughter not known what to do? How would that have changed her life and our family's life?

Even more concerning was whether this could happen to my daughter again. Could there be even a more nefarious entity that could successfully take possession of my vibrant six-year-old?

When I got home that morning from dropping my girls off at school, I crumbled. I cried. I begged God for help. I was beyond exhausted. There were months of sleepless nights. I learned right away that all of these beings and entities don't need sleep. I was scared. Well, I was more terrified than scared, and I couldn't show anyone how terrified I truly was. Being scared gets your adrenaline pumping. Being terrified can be paralyzing.

This was my very own private hell. There was no one I could talk to about it in any depth, partly because it was so crazy and partly because I was having a tough time wrapping my head around all of this.

## We Were a Normal Family

Sometimes, I think back to the days when I thought just getting up, getting ready for school, and dealing with our jobs, friends, and the day-to-day was its own challenge. Now, I look at those days as blissful, simple, and easy times. What happened to us? How did our lives become so weird, crazy, and unexplainable?

I was a middle school teacher, and my husband was a business consultant. I volunteered a lot for our school and community. I'm somewhat civic-minded and worked on political campaigns at the local city and school levels. My husband was responsible for the local school's "Dad's Club." He coached kids' soccer. Together, we spent our weekends tag teaming to make sure each of our daughters got to their games and events on time. I spent countless hours helping with homework at the dinner table. We were always busy doing ordinary family activities.

Then, one day, all of this changed. It was like a switch was flipped. We now had a family secret. A secret so strange, so unusual, and downright terrifying that it had a tight grip on my family. Every day held a new adventure when it came to this secret, and I never got a heads up on what the next adventure would be because, well, my imagination isn't *that* good.

The only certainty I could count on was exhaustion. My family and I had learned the importance of living two separate lives. Many of our friends, up until recently, had no idea of the private hell that we were going through all these past years.

What we were experiencing was not something we could share with anyone, not family, friends, colleagues, doctors, or therapists. What we were experiencing came right out of a horror movie from Hollywood. The only difference was this horror was our new normal, and it was no movie.

Over the next two years, our house became what I termed a "Ghost Super-Highway." I had no clue what to do with our new and unwanted houseguests. I had no idea we could have that many in our house. I mean, there were hundreds, if not thousands, of ghosts coming and going all the time. It was as if my daughter and I had become a ghost magnet, and I had no idea what to do about it. No idea how to help us, no idea how to protect us or shield us from all of this. They all wanted her attention, 24 hours a day and seven days a week.

Why? Because ghosts don't need to sleep. Why were they bothering us? What did they want from us? Somehow, we became a bright light to them, like moths to a flame.

They pestered her constantly for attention. There was never a break, and it was taking its toll on my mental and physical health. One important concept I learned early on was death does not change a soul's personality. Not all of these ghosts that came into our home were nice. If you were a jerk in life, you would be a jerk in death.

# THE GHOST CHILD WHO WANTED
# MY DAUGHTER TO DIE

It was around one in the morning when I heard it. I ran down the hall so fast that I felt teleported there. Did someone break into our house? Was there a fire? Or was it something paranormal? I had no idea what was about to come out of her mouth. When I got to her room, I found her crouched in the corner of her bed, pressed up against the wall and in the fetal position. My heart was racing, and I could feel the adrenaline coursing through my veins.

"What happened? Are you all right?" I asked her in a loud whisper. The rest of our family was still sleeping, and at this point, I had gotten good at sleeping with one eye open, so to speak.

"I was sleeping when Annabelle started poking me," said my daughter. "When I woke up, she was standing over me with this big butcher knife. She said she was going to do more than poke me with it. She said she is going to stab me with it!" she screamed.

I often longed for the simple days when Annabelle was not angry and violent. Never in my wildest dreams would

I have ever predicted that my family and I would live in a house of horrors.

As a schoolteacher, I knew how to handle children. I spent 15 years in the classroom. But Annabelle was an entirely different story. Annabelle was a ghost child. And ghosts play by different rules. I found myself constantly vacillating between feeling sorry for her and wanting to help her, yet at the same time being so angry with her that I literally couldn't see straight.

My anger intensified toward her behavior as she escalated against my six-year-old daughter, who could not defend herself. How do you reason with a ghost? At the same time, I also felt deep compassion for this trapped soul. Not only was I trying to stabilize my daughter's health and well-being, but I was also sorting through my own conflicting emotions of rage, sorrow, and even love toward this ghostly child.

I mean, what if my child had died and somehow became stuck between dimensions as a ghost and was lost, scared, and lonely?

As a mom, that thought was even more chilling than if one of my kids had died. My family lived a delicate juggling act of pretending to be normal with jobs, school, and friends while learning to handle a real live ghost who harmed my daughter. I didn't realize then what a toll this experience had taken on our loving, regular lives. We were all so vulnerable and naive.

I had no idea how she found my daughter. She just came home with her one day after school. I remembered my daughter telling my husband and me about her new friend.

We just looked at one another as if we were reading each other's minds. "Is this what an imaginary friend is?" "This is so nuts!" "Is this normal?" "What should we do about this?" "What if our daughter tells her *living* friends about Annabelle?" "What do we do with this ghost child?" "Can things get any crazier?" "Can we make her leave, and if so, where would she go?"

In the beginning, they quickly became the best of friends: my daughter, a living child, and this ghost child. I could hear constant one-sided giggles and full-blown belly laughs coming from my daughter's bedroom on a daily basis.

But then there were moments of silence and sadness.

No one ever said being a parent would be easy, but being a parent to a psychic child was not easy. It's unnerving to have such little control over such a strange situation as a parent. Annabelle could say or do anything to my daughter, and I would be clueless.

"I miss my mommy. You are so lucky you have a mommy," Annabelle would say to her between sobs. "I wish I had a mom like yours."

This had a direct impact on all of my children. I was making dinner one night when my daughter approached me and said, "Mom, I feel so bad for Annabelle. I can't imagine my life without you. How does someone grow up without a *mom?*"

But the sad irony was that Annabelle would never have a chance to grow up. She was stuck here as a ghost, and I had no idea what to do about it. At the same time, Annabelle's situation also made me appreciate my family all the more.

"I don't know," I said. "Sometimes people are forced into a situation, and there is nothing anyone can do about it." This was the only answer I could give her.

My daughter often would find Annabelle crying in her room at our house. She was so homesick for her own family that we could all feel her sorrow. It was as if her sadness permeated the walls of our house, leaving us all feeling melancholy and sad. It was wild how we could all feel such strong emotions coming from this little ghost girl.

She wanted to go home and be with her mom, but this was impossible. And I needed to figure out how to help her.

There were many times when Annabelle would wrap her arms and legs around me and hug me, telling me she loved me like she loved her own mom. Sometimes, she would ask me if she could step on my feet so she could 'walk' with, or rather, on me.

"Annabelle loves this! She says it is so much fun, mom!" My daughter would tell me. I have to admit, it was a bit strange, but this whole situation was beyond bizarre.

She and my daughter spent hours each day playing and talking. She would go to school with my daughter and spend her days with the other children in her class. One day after school, Annabelle and my daughter asked me if I could help them to find Annabelle's mom. I told her I had no idea how to find her mom. I did not know her last name, and neither did Annabelle. She just kept talking about her mommy.

I had already searched my local area and news for car accidents and found nothing. It was then that I realized an important fact that I had been completely missing these long months: Annabelle had no idea she was dead.

I somehow had to figure out how to break this news to this little girl gently.

"Annabelle, honey, do you remember when you first came to us and told us you were in a car accident?" I asked. "Do you remember what happened?"

"Not really," said Annabelle. "I heard my mommy say we're going home after being at a party. It was late at night because I had already put on my pajamas. My mommy, daddy, and I were at my aunt's house celebrating her birthday. We stayed really late and, on the way home, I fell asleep in the car. I remember waking up because my dad was screaming at another driver. I think the driver speeded through a red light.

"The next thing I knew, I saw my dad's car, and it was really mangled up. I could see the car from up high- like I was looking down on the car like I was floating. I then saw fire trucks, police, and ambulances. I could see my mommy crying and yelling, and a police officer was holding her. She was screaming so loud and... and there was another police officer holding my daddy back.

"My daddy kept trying to get back to the car, and he was screaming, 'Nooooo! Anna! Anna! My baby!' over and over. He was trying to get to me. But the car was so smashed up they could not get me out. They had to wait for this tool, this thing that looked like giant scissors, to get me out. I. . . I guess I forgot about all of this. It was so scary and so sad. I miss my mommy and daddy so much. Where did they go? Where are my mommy and daddy?" Annabelle asked.

Annabelle became quiet as if a sickening reality began to awaken within her.

"Annabelle, sweetie," I said. "Do you know what *really* happened? You died that night in that car accident. This is why you can't find your parents. Do you know you are dead?"

It was unimaginable to me that this little girl, who had been with us for almost a year at this point, had no clue that she was dead. She was a ghost. Annabelle never said another word for the rest of that day.

My daughter was so worried about her. How does one console a grieving ghost child? Or any grieving ghost, for that matter? Children look to adults for guidance, but what kind of guidance do I offer a ghost child?

## Annabelle's Rage

As I stated, in the beginning, she started out friendly enough. Something must have snapped inside when she realized her plight because all of a sudden, sweet Annabelle was now not so sweet. She became full of rage, a rage that I had never experienced before from a living person, much less a dead person. Annabelle was furious that she no longer had a mom, that she could never go home, and that her own mom could never again hug, kiss, or tuck her into bed at night.

How do I describe my terror? Any conscientious parent knows it's hard enough to protect their children from the everyday physical world and known dangers out there, but how does a parent protect their child from beings and entities that most people can't see?

In the past, I could use my "mom voice" to scold Annabelle, trying to exert some authority over this ghost child. It worked in the beginning. But now that she had realized she was dead, she had a new and chilling awareness about her.

How do you reprimand a ghost? After all, they really don't have to play by the same rules.

The reality was that I no longer had control over her. It wasn't like I could put her in time-out or take away a favorite toy. I could demand that she leave, but that wouldn't mean she'd obey. But what would make her go, and where would she go? She was still a little girl but not my child. I could exert some authority over her if she were a living child. But she was not a living child; I had no authority over her, and she knew it.

This realization Annabelle had was because I was the one who told her she had died. Because I told her she was dead, something in her soul snapped, and she now felt she had free reign.

"Annabelle, what on earth are you doing," I asked. "We need to sleep. Why are you trying to scare my daughter? What do you have to say for yourself?" Annabelle could always hear me. Annabelle's response was bone-chilling.

"I want YOU to die!" she told my daughter. "It's not fair that you get to have a mom and... and I don't! I hate you! I hate you!" Annabelle screamed at her.

As a parent, that was a chilling thought. Can a ghost harm the living? Annabelle's poking of my daughter brought my fear to new heights. So far, Annabelle and the myriad of other ghosts and entities in our house only managed to keep waking her and me at night when we slept. Sleep was now becoming a precious commodity, and I would soon find the answer to my question.

"Annabelle, I know you miss your mom and your family," I said. "I want to help you, but I don't know how. I don't know what to do for you, and I feel horrible about your situation. No one deserves what you are going through. But here we are. We all need to sleep and get up in the morning to go to work and school. I can't have you scaring people at night or any other time. Do you understand me?"

She started to cry and hugged my leg. It gave me hope that I got through to her. But that hope didn't last long. I never went back to sleep that night. My husband and I were now terrified of this ghost child.

What could she do to our daughter?

## The Reign of Terror Begins

It was about 7 p.m., and that meant it was time to get ready for bed. My daughter was showering when I heard her shrieking from the bathroom. She came running out with shampoo in her hair and a towel around her. The shampoo was now stinging her eyes, and she was hysterical and shaking.

"What happened?" I asked her.

"I...I got in the shower and turned around, and Annabelle was there holding a knife," she said. "Annabelle told me she was going to stab me in the back, and I told her not to do it. Then she stabbed me in the back THREE times! I felt it, and it hurt! It hurt, Mom!"

I looked at her back, and my heart just sank. It was everything I could do to not show any fear to my daughter or Annabelle. I could visibly see and feel three red welts on her back in places that she could not have self-inflicted. My daughter was not lying, and according to my daughter, Annabelle was nowhere to be found. She knew I would be angry with her

This became the normal shower routine for my daughter. For months, every time my daughter would take a shower, Annabelle would stab her with this etheric knife. This would always leave marks on her back, over and over. I was at a loss as to how to protect her. And knowing I could not protect her left a constant pit of fear swelling up in my gut.

For months, I sat on the bathroom floor every night while she showered to try to prevent Annabelle from hurting her. Often, even that didn't work. I will never fully understand this. How does a ghost child get a butcher knife? How can she cause visible, physical harm to a living person?

I needed help now more than ever. My constant and chronic search for help never yielded any sustainable results. I felt like a complete failure. I made it my full-time job to look for help that would, well, actually be helpful. I needed to reclaim our home. We needed to be able to sleep at night. We needed to feel a bit of happiness again. Every time I searched for answers, I ended up at a dead end. Annabelle was not the only ghost or being taking up residency in our home. There were many others.

As we approached the fall season again, Annabelle found a new way to torture my daughter: through our pets.

She delighted in torturing our house-trained rabbit, Benny. Benny was the sweetest and most adorable creature, and Annabelle enjoyed chasing him around the house with her knife.

Rabbits don't have vocal cords, and he would make these odd throaty sounds and thump his foot against the wood floor, trying to get my or anyone in my family's attention to help save him from the wrath of Annabelle. I would scoop him up and hold him tight when this happened. I felt so bad for Benny. This little rabbit did deserve better. He was now living in a constant state of fear, cowering in corners of the house while Annabelle stood over him.

Despite what was happening to my daughter and Benny, for some reason, Annabelle had not begun to harm any other family member physically. I was grateful for that.

It was a Wednesday, the short day at school when school would let out early. I picked up my kids l, and when we got home, Annabelle made a bold statement to my daughter.

"I want your mom to be my mom, and I want YOU TO BE DEAD!" My daughter reported to me in hysterical tears. Annabelle ordered my daughter to leave and move out. If she didn't, she would continue to harm her and our other pets.

At this time, the ever-present giant pit of worry and fear that never left my stomach was getting more significant. I didn't think that was possible. I worked hard to shield our other daughters from this nightmare. They couldn't see or hear what their sister could; if they did, that would worsen matters. I also needed to make sure my husband could sleep at night so he could function at work the next day because I ended up leaving my job, and he was now the sole provider for our family.

During this entire time, I was searching for help, but help still eluded me. How does one remove a ghost? What does it mean to remove them? If I banished her, would she then become someone else's problem? The other issue was that, in the end, this is a little girl who is lost, scared, and lonely.

How could I possibly fix that?

## The Saddest Birthday

Childhood birthdays are supposed to be full of family and friend celebrations, cakes, parties, and presents. A couple of weeks before our daughter's birthday, I asked her what she wanted to do.

"Do you want to have friends over for your birthday," I asked her. "Do you want to go out to dinner as a family? Do you want me to make lemon cupcakes and bring them to school?"

"Lemon cupcakes, and I want to go to the pizza place for dinner!" She squealed with excitement.

That was my mistake. I didn't realize that Annabelle was listening to this conversation. I should have known better.

"If I can't have a birthday, if I can't have a birthday cake and presents," said Annabelle. "If I can't have my mommy on MY birthday, neither can you. I hate you! I hate you! I hate you! You don't deserve to have a birthday. It's not FAIR! I'm going to kill you so you can't have another birthday just like me."

This became Annabelle's nightly bedtime mantra to my daughter. Imagine trying to fall asleep to that terrifying threat.

Annabelle repeatedly screamed this at my daughter every day and night for over a week before her birthday. That's when my sweet little girl came crying to me out of fear and exhaustion. Our daughter just wanted a break from the torture and harassment that was never-ending. She just wanted to be happy.

All I wanted to do was to promise my little girl that she would have the best birthday ever, but that would have been a false promise, and I could not lie to her as much as I had wanted to.

As time went on, Annabelle stopped listening and obeying me, and there was nothing I could do about it. Annabelle was sucking the life out of us. Ghosts don't need sleep because there is no time in that dimension. This is how the dead exhaust the living by harassing them 24 hours a day.

I found myself terrified as well. This ghost child was already stabbing my daughter in the shower on a nightly basis. What else could she be capable of doing? I was becoming increasingly frantic to find a way out of this living hell caused by this seven-year-old ghost child.

"So, you think you're going to have a birthday party at school, do you," said Annabelle. "You have no friends, so why are you bringing cupcakes?"

This vile little ghost child whispered in my daughter's ear over and over, and she started to believe she had no friends. This psychological warfare with this ghost child kept growing.

Annabelle taunted my daughter as she and I made lemon cupcakes with lemon frosting the afternoon before her birthday. It is hard to be stoic when you have not slept in months. I found myself doubting my ability to protect my child, questioning my skills as a parent, and feeling like a failure. I had run out of ways to protect and help her. I tried to ignore Annabelle and worked hard to help my daughter ignore her, too.

But ignoring a problem never changes anything.

How can you put on a good face with school friends, neighbors, and co-workers when nothing in your world feels normal? This is especially true when you have to pretend to the outside world that all is fine within your life when nothing is fine.

When you haven't slept in so long, you justify that two consecutive hours of sleep is enough to be considered a full night's sleep. As a former schoolteacher, I knew my daughter's chronic fatigue, the huge dark circles under her eyes, her many absences, and her chronic late arrivals to school were drawing unwanted attention to us.

On the morning of her birthday, I let her sleep in and go to school an hour late again. The attendance secretary gave me 'that look' as I checked her in. I lied. I told the secretary she had a bad headache, and she just rolled her eyes at me. We both knew that was a lie. But the truth would have been worse. "Yeah, the ghost child that lives with us was harassing her all night again." That conversation would not have ended well.

We got to the classroom with the lemon cupcakes, and I asked the teacher if they could sing Happy Birthday to her during morning recess, and her teacher agreed. I also told her teacher she had a bad headache and may need to leave early. The teacher's response made me uneasy.

"Of course," said her teacher. "But I think we need to schedule a parent-teacher conference. She has been missing a lot of school and has not been herself lately, and I am worried about her."

This comment instilled more fear in me than Annabelle had ever created. I was petrified about Child Protective Services calling me about our daughter with a welfare check, and it would have included our other two daughters, as well. How does a parent explain to a government official who has the power to take away your child that she is being haunted by the dead and a bunch of other dark entities that I have no idea what they are? How do I explain ghosts don't need sleep or about the chronic nightly harassment that we have been enduring for over a year? Child Protective Services would probably certify me as an unfit parent and take my kids and drug the psychic one.

I stayed at the school, not wanting to be far from her in case Annabelle pulled a stunt on my daughter. I busied myself with some volunteer work in the copy room. It was only an hour until recess. I had hoped she could make it through without falling asleep at her desk or getting attacked by Annabelle.

She, or rather we, did not sleep for one minute that night. Anabelle's rage was at epic proportions. At this point, I could feel Annabelle stabbing and poking me! If I ever doubted this was real (which I never did), I now knew beyond a doubt that it was indeed genuine. And it very much hurt and left welts.

At recess, everyone sang Happy Birthday and hugged her, and Annabelle watched the whole thing. After recess, my exhausted little birthday girl asked, "Can I go home yet?"

I took her out of school around 10:15 a.m. and told her we should celebrate at a nearby restaurant for a birthday breakfast. We were starving, yet we were too tired to chew. The truth was neither of us wanted to go home. Home was hell. We ordered breakfast and sat in this booth for a long time.

My heart broke for my little girl. Here we were, sitting in this restaurant, afraid to go home, too tired to eat, and having missed another day at school. But despite these bizarre events, one triumph had never occurred to me.

"I got to go to school, and everyone *did* sing happy birthday to me, and I *do* have friends. Annabelle was wrong!" She cried with glee, and with that, for a few moments, we were both happy. It was a small victory. But a victory, nonetheless.

Once home, we both crawled into my bed and passed out for almost eight hours. It had been at least six months since we both slept that long and that hard. Another small victory!

We both felt amazingly refreshed from all that sleep— eight hours more than we had gotten in the past week!

The family went to dinner that night to celebrate her birthday, and we had a good time. After dinner, our birthday girl made an announcement.

"No one is ever allowed to say the name Annabelle ever again. That is what I want for my birthday."

## How Do You Get Rid of a Ghost?

As time passed, Annabelle stopped listening and obeying me, and I could do nothing about it. Annabelle was sucking the life out of us. Ghosts don't need sleep because there is no time in that dimension. This is how the dead exhaust the living by harassing them 24 hours a day.

*How do you get rid of a ghost?* This was the one question that kept coming back to me repeatedly. As I mentioned in the beginning, I had been searching for help. But help kept eluding me. It seemed like an eternity of terror, fear, and hopelessness.

Annabelle was not the only ghost who came into my home. To make this story more complicated, a myriad of other ghosts and dark entities were constantly after both of us. I felt they were licking their chops to get at us as if we were a tasty morsel they wanted to own.

# THE RITE AID HOBOS

It was the golden hour at our home. In the early part of the evening, when the house was picked up, the kids were in bed, and we could relax a bit after a full day. However, relaxing was becoming more of a luxury than normal family living. It seemed like we were always on high alert for some impending doom to arrive. We just weren't privy to what that happening would be. The hard part about this is it keeps you off balance, never knowing when the next psychic or paranormal action will hit you.

"They're back. I can smell the cigarette smoke," my husband said.

"I know. I'm just as tired of this as you are," I said. "Why can't we just sit down at the end of the day and watch television for an hour like a normal family? I think they are standing to the left of the television set. At least that's where I think the smoke is coming from."

"I suppose it's better than dealing with Annabelle or Prissy, the hat man. At least these guys smoke cigarettes and leave us alone," he said.

He was referring to the Rite Aid Hobos, as we started calling them. They were back and had been coming and going for a few months. They never really stayed that long, but we always knew their presence because our house smelled like cigarette smoke.

The Rite Aid Hobos were a trio of ghosts who probably died of substance abuse. I noticed them a while back and commented that I would always see them in front of the Rite Aid store. They told me they spent most of their time hanging out in the store's liquor section, and then at night, they would be out front just watching people.

"Mom, are those the Rite Aid Hobos?" my daughter asked as she walked into the room. "They say they want to play video games."

"What," I said. "We don't have any video games. We need to ask them why they are here and how they got here."

My little interdimensional translator was back to work, even though her real work should have been doing her homework at this point in the evening. But sometimes, I needed help in figuring this out. How is it these guys got here? Why are they here? How can we get them to leave?

"Mom, they say that they are friends and like to hang out at Rite Aid because they like to scare the people that go into the store," she explained. "The small one is telling me that the best ones to scare are the drunk ones that go in to buy liquor.

"They can also tell them what booze to buy, and they will make bets on if the person does what they say. The drunk ones are the easiest to scare, and they love doing it," she said. I watched her eyes get big. "He says that when the living people are really drunk, they can go inside their bodies and get drunk with them."

"Interesting. Since we don't have alcohol and we don't have video games, and we aren't afraid of them, why are they here?" I asked.

"The small one seems to do the talking for them. He says that they saw our van, and it glowed, and they were curious about that. So, they followed us home. They say that you and I glow, and our house feels warm to them," she said.

"Great. More ghosts and these ghosts smoke," I said.

"I demand you all to stop smoking RIGHT NOW," said my daughter. "This is a non-smoking house. You can smoke at Rite Aid. You can't stay here."

"Oh, so sorry. We didn't mean to. . . We like it here and don't want to cause trouble. We'll leave," the small ghost told my daughter.

Then, in an instant, they were gone. I was surprised that they left so quickly.

However, my surprise quickly waned as we discovered that they would come and go at their own free will and they would continue to smoke. I guess they realized that we had no power over them. That's when they knew they could come and go as they pleased. We told them repeatedly to leave and go back to Rite Aid. Occasionally, they would comply.

What unnerved me is that these ghosts told us how they could enter another person's body and that it's easier to do when the living person is drunk. If this were the case, how easy is it for a ghost to possess a person who is a substance abuser? Could this explain multiple personality disorders? Could this also explain why addictions may be so hard to kick?

I didn't know, but these are fair questions.

# LITTLE BOY LOST

"That's me! That's me!" he shouted at my daughter.

The two of us were watching TV that Friday night. It was one of those rare quiet nights. My husband took the other two girls to a bookstore with our neighbors, and it was just the two of us, or at least that's what I thought until this Dateline promo came on during the commercials.

"Who's here, and who are you talking to?" I asked my daughter.

"It's that boy who was on the Dateline commercial, Mom," she said. "He's here! He says he's not missing and that he's right here. He is really excited he's on TV. He says he's never been on TV before. He's really talkative, mom. He wants to know what station this is."

"It's NBC, Channel 7," I said. "Do you want to talk with him?"

"Yes. He's so funny and nice," she said.

"Please ask him how he got here," I said. I contemplated yet another ghost coming into our home and wondering how these apparitions kept finding us. This was my million-dollar question that I could never quite figure out.

My mind reeled as I tried to count how many ghosts we had seen or spoken to. I just couldn't track anymore. I was so tired. If they were living people, we would be in constant fire code violations for having too many people in a small space. My thoughts were interrupted by my little dimensional translator, who started talking to our newest friend.

"He says he just popped in when the commercial came on," she said. "He has no idea how he did this. But he's super excited I can talk to him. He says he's been really scared and lonely and misses his mommy and dad."

"What happened to him? Does he know," I asked.

The severity of this situation just seemed to magnify in my mind. What on earth? I now have this murdered little boy in my living room, and the entire country is fixated on finding him. No one knows what happened to him. According to the news story on TV, the authorities have not found his body. They aren't even sure if he's dead or alive.

I could imagine that this must be a parent's worst nightmare, knowing that your baby, your child, suddenly went missing. You think about that empty bed at night. You then wonder if they are cold at night. You secretly hope they aren't hungry, cold, or lost, but that deep gnawing feeling won't leave. You're not ready to accept death, and you desperately want to fight and protect your child, but you can't.

I felt the hopelessness of this boy's mom and dad. A missing child? All of those unanswered questions that will haunt a parent for the rest of their life. . . Oh, and Annabelle is still with us, causing all sorts of problems.

"And any time you want to stop, just let me know. I know this can be tiring," I told my daughter.

"Mom, I got this," she said. "He is a nice boy, and I want to help him. Plus, he's way nicer than Annabelle!"

The boy started to tell his story. "My step-mom took me to school early because I had to set up for the science fair. I wanted to look my best, and I was taking too long, and she got super duper mad at me. I just wanted to look my best. Do you know what my project was on? It was on tree frogs. Did you know some tree frogs have green bodies? Some have blue bodies, and some have red bodies. Someday, I want to touch a real one!"

My munchkin translator was talking so fast I could barely keep up as I was taking notes. Somehow, I felt this was important to do.

## Tree Frog Validation

This little boy went on and on. He was so excited to share his knowledge on tree frogs, where they lived, what they ate, and all kinds of other tree frog facts that my daughter had no clue about. There was no way she would have known any of this.

This validated the reality of our odd situation. I wished I had a recorder to capture the audio of this conversation word for word.

"Ask him why he left the school. Did something happen?" I asked.

I had no idea what was going to happen next.

"He says that his step-mom said she was sorry for being angry at him and that he should set his stuff inside and come back, and she would take him for some ice cream," she said. "But they didn't get ice cream. He says he got back in the car and asked about the ice cream, and then she got really mad at him again and started screaming at him."

My daughter started crying. "How can people be so mean? He's such a nice boy!"

"Do you need to stop for now?" I asked her.

Very calmly, she replies, "No. He needs our help. I can do this."

Many times, during our experiences with these ghosts and entities, I marveled at her bravery. Her adult-like maturity and actions surpassed her actual Earth years.

"I'm asking him what happened," she said. "He says that she was yelling at him and ripped his glasses off of him and threw them down on the floor of the car. She wouldn't let him pick them up, and he can't see very well without them."

I notice my daughter pausing and staring at the TV. The Dateline show is on, and she said he wants to watch it with her. I listened as the show was going over possible areas where his body may be located.

"I am not near the water," shouted the boy. "Oh, they are close, but they need to go to the other side of the street into the golden field. I am not in the water. Why do they keep thinking I'm in the water?" My daughter said the boy was screaming and jumping up and down.

"Mom, he wants to show me what happened," she said.

Events were happening so fast now, and before I could comprehend the news, my daughter went into some sort of trance. She was staring off into space. Her voice shifted a bit as she became very still. It scared the hell out of me.

I knew by now that I had to be highly attentive to her. I moved closer. As she stood by the couch, I wanted to reach for her arm, but I held back, afraid. Yet I wanted to keep her as grounded as possible. I didn't have the experience to steer my daughter through this.

The only tool I had to keep her as safe as possible was my intuition. There was no psychic parenting handbook to help guide me through this bizarre situation. I had to listen to my intuition and rely upon all my physical and intellectual instincts that I acquired up to this point, which wasn't much.

My daughter explained that she sees herself in the car with him. What the heck did that mean? I wanted to pull her out of this trance, but I couldn't. Somehow, her psychic ability was transporting her to another time and location.

"I need you to keep talking me through what is always happening. I need to know you're safe," I said.

"He's taking me for a ride in the car," she said. "I can see his stepmom, and she is big and mean and ugly. She stops the car and tells him to get out. He wants his glasses. But she tells him no. He's really, really scared mom. OH MY GOD!" She screamed.

I could see her react and feel that events had suddenly changed.

"He's showing me he's bleeding in his stomach," she said. "His stepmom shot him or stabbed him! He's not sure. Mom, he was so shocked. He never thought she would kill him. Blood is pouring out of him. Oh my God, mom."

My daughter fearlessly continued reciting to me the events as if they appeared to her in real time. I didn't fully understand how she could do that feat, but I was convinced it was real.

"How can someone do that to a little boy," she asked. "He's showing me that his step-mom drove far off the road in the car. It might be a dirt road or not even a road," she said.

"Was your stepmom's friend with her? Did she help in any way?" I asked them both, as the Dateline story theorized she may have had a female accomplice.

"No. She wasn't there," she said.

When he was done showing my daughter what had happened, the three of us came together with the realization that we were all witnesses to a real-life murder. We saw the horror of knowing that this little boy was violently murdered at the hands of his trusted stepmom, who was in his care, which was beyond sad.

Being a witness, even second-hand, to the murder of a child was not part of my world. I grappled with the reality of this horrific situation as it was confirmed on the news show.

As a mom, how could I possibly understand intentionally murdering their own child? I couldn't, and I wouldn't. I had to do something, but what? As a teacher in the physical world, I am bound by law to report any form of child abuse or neglect. But I was not dealing in the physical world anymore with this little boy. Yet, I knew it was as real as anything I had ever seen as a teacher.

The emotional toll of recanting the events that led up to his death left us all exhausted.

I realized that my little girl just witnessed a murder first-hand. Plus, I now had all of these intimate details about this crime. I had to think about what to do with this information. I needed to talk to my husband in private about all of this.

During my frenzied state of mind at these events, I somehow was able to take notes. Looking back, those were copious notes. I was so afraid I would forget something.

"How about the two of you sit on the sofa with me?" I asked. "Let's cuddle for a bit. I am so sorry this happened to you. You are a wonderful little boy." I knew he could hear me.

"You are so lucky. You have such a nice mom," this little boy told my daughter, who relayed it to me.

"My mom is nice, too. I miss her, and I wish she could hear me," he said. "Thank you for being my friend. I miss my friends. They are all so sad. I can hear them and see them, but they can't see me. Can I stay here with you tonight? I usually go to my mom's house at night, and I run up and down the stairs, hoping she can hear me. But she cries. She cries all the time. I'll go back to her house tomorrow night." He told my daughter.

"Please tell him he can come over any time. I want to figure out how to help him." I told her.

We were all so tired. Every day was a new adventure. Every day, there was some new significant happening that I tried to identify. I decided that I would call their local police department in the morning. If I could give them this information and his murder was solved, would this help him to cross over into Heaven? He was so sad, cold, and lonely. I couldn't bear it. I had no idea how any of this worked. We knew in our heart of hearts that this little boy was kind and sweet, and he needed our help.

"Mom, he wants to go to school with me. Can he? Can he go with me?" She was so excited.

"You both realize that if he goes to school with you, you can't talk to him around ANYBODY, right?" I told them both.

The situation with Annabelle had drained us both, and the school was still suspicious that my daughter was okay. Thinking through the pitfalls of being exposed, I knew that we couldn't have my daughter act anything but normal at school. It would raise more questions that we couldn't answer, especially since Annabelle still tormented my daughter at school by pushing her in class or causing her to yell out in surprise.

This lost little boy seemed refreshingly different, so I reluctantly let him attend school with my daughter.

"We know, mom." She answered for both of them.

## Contacting The Police

I got them and my other two daughters off to school and then headed back home to make a phone call. I had to figure out what to say. There were many conversations I had in my head playing out this scenario.

*The initial conversation in my head looked like this: "Hi, Portland PD. So, this Dateline show was on last night, and your missing boy stopped by. Oh, he's a ghost now, and he was talking to my daughter and told her that his stepmom did it."*

*"What's that? Oh, my daughter is seven years old. She talks to dead people all the time."* Yeah, that would have gone over well.

As soon as I returned, I looked up the phone number for the Portland Police Department. We all wanted this horrid situation resolved. I took a deep breath and rehearsed the story in my head again. I was scared. I had to pretend that it was me and not my daughter, who was a minor, who spoke with this ghost boy. I could not jeopardize Child

Protective Services coming by and taking away my child. As a public school teacher, I knew the potential reality should this get out.

The other issue I faced was I had all this first-hand knowledge. What if, by some bizarre set of circumstances, they thought I was somehow involved? But I had to make this call. I promised this little boy I would do my best, and in his world, the adults in his life failed him.

I was not about to be another adult who failed him.

I summoned the courage to make this call, and there was a pre-recorded message stating if you were calling about this case and were a psychic or anything along those terms, to hang up. Those types of calls were not welcome. Rather anticlimactic.

When I picked up my daughter and this little boy that afternoon, I gave them the news. He was so sad about this it broke my heart. He asked if he could spend the days with us and spend the nights at his mom's house. Of course, I said yes. I mean, really, how could I say no to that request?

It was at this moment that I had a huge epiphany and many more questions. The epiphany was I understand the concept of imaginary friends- they aren't so imaginary.

I now had other questions about how all of this works. How was it that this little ghost boy, who had been dead for only a few months, was able to travel to our house and to his mom's house, which is a thousand miles away? How does the energy of ghosts work? Why do they keep coming to our house? How can I help this little boy?

He can't seem to cross over, and I don't know how to help him. But at least I knew he was safe here for now.

# THE BIRTHDAY SUIT

O ne sunny southern California afternoon, we headed to a family friend's house to drop off an item I promised. To this day, I can't remember what we were dropping off, and it doesn't really matter. I remember it was a hot summer day, and my daughters came in with me as it was too hot to have them stay in the car. Plus, they looked forward to playing with friends they hadn't seen in a while.

"Hey, Tim, how's it going," I asked him as he opened the door.

"Good, Laura, come on in. Do you want something to drink," he asked.

"Sure, thanks." No sooner had I uttered those words than my daughter's eyes bugged out of her head. Her reaction told me there was unusual activity going on in this house. I had no idea what it was because I still couldn't see what she could see.

I knew this: Tim and his family had no idea we kept a paranormal family secret. As Tim was preparing our iced tea, I asked my daughter what was going on. Tim was a police officer and didn't work in the nicest areas. He was good at his job, and community outreach was always important to him. To this day, he's a great guy, and so is his family.

"There's a ghost with Tim," she said.

"Ok, so what's the big deal?" I asked her.

He's NAKED and really, really FAT," her nervous attempt at a whisper was so loud it hurt my ear. "Ewwww," she said while making gagging and barfing noises.

"What does he look like," I asked, trying not to laugh.

"Mom! Stop it! You're not funny," she said.

I was rather curious as to what my daughter was seeing. How bad was this? Then Tim walked in. I told my daughter to play with her sister and friends.

Tim walked back into the room with our drinks. "So, what's new in your world, Tim?" I probed him, secretly hoping to find out why there was this fat naked guy in his house.

"Not much," he said. He's a man of few words, but when he speaks, people listen.

"Anything exciting happen today at work?" I asked, hoping for a longer answer than a simple yes or no. I was curious. Why was there a fat, naked ghost hanging out with him? I mean, seriously, this must be the funniest paranormal issue we had so far. Frankly, I was kind of enjoying the moment. When you live in chronic fear, chronic unknowingness, and chronic exhaustion, a bit of levity can help bring you back into balance. At least, that's how I justified this as a comical situation.

That's when my daughter walked back into the living room. "He's still here," she whispered in my ear as she hugged me. I have to admit, she's getting clever at disguising communications when it comes to the family secret.

"Today, I had a call to go to this apartment," said Tim. "One of the neighbors said there was a powerfully foul smell. And do you know what that means?"

"I think I do, but I don't want to know. So, what happened," I asked him.

"The apartment manager let me into this apartment," said Tim. "And let me tell you, the person who lived there was a hoarder of epic proportions. There was stuff piled high to the ceiling. As I walked into the living room, there was so much stuff in there that you had to walk a path to get around. There were car parts in the bathtub. Who stockpiles car parts in their bathtub?" He all of a sudden became very chatty.

"Wow," I said while waiting for him to get to the good part. I felt like I knew what was coming.

"The smell in this place was beyond horrid, beyond disgusting," said Tim. "We kept walking through the place, room by room. The bedroom was full of trash bags filled with used food containers. I swear, this was so odd. Then I walked into the kitchen, and there he was." His voice trailed off.

"There was who?" I asked.

"This huge and very naked man," he said. "He was spread out -- half of him was on the floor, and the other half was on piles of old magazines and newspapers. He was 350 pounds of pure nakedness. I suspect he had a heart attack and had been dead for a couple of days. This was not a pretty sight. I swear, I don't get paid enough at times. I mean, this is something I can never, ever unsee. You know what I mean? This image of what I found. . . it's like it's etched in my brain," he said, half-laughing.

"I have a not-so-random question for you. And this question is out in left field. Do you believe in ghosts?" I very hesitantly asked him.

Because of the comical nature of this situation and because our families have been friends for years, it was an excellent opportunity to test the waters despite my initial reluctance.

"I have seen some bizarre and unexplainable things on the job. So yes, ghosts, I do believe they exist," he said.

"Well, I need to tell you something," I said. "That fat naked guy you found in the apartment today? Well, he's standing right next to you." And then I just started laughing and laughing.

A part of me felt bad that I was laughing at this naked ghostly stranger, but at the same time, the pressures my family had been living with were just awful. It was as if I was inside a pressure cooker, and the addition of this fat, naked ghost released this pressure valve that had been building up inside of me all this time.

"What?! You're kidding!? Oh my God, what do I do? How did he get here, in my home," he said, a bit freaked.

"Well, lucky for you, I now know how to take care of that," I said, as I had recently learned how to cross over the dead. And with that, I crossed him over. He was one of the first ghosts I had learned to cross over.

In addition to the whole naked issue, this true ghost story is memorable because I have since learned to cross over the dead. Surprisingly, the task was easy for me while my personal growth expanded. Ghosts tend to be "period pieces." This means people who see ghosts see what they are wearing at the time of death and anchor that soul in that moment.

Ghosts stay stuck in time. A ghost from the 1800's looks very different from one from the 1200's or 1962.

This guy died in his birthday suit, and that was what he was wearing when he died -- bare, nude, nada, nothing. I do kind of wish I would have asked him what he was doing in his kitchen naked, but I didn't.

Moral of the story: If you think you might die, make sure you change your underwear and put on your best clothes. Just like Mom told you.

# PREMONITIONS AND
# MY PERSONAL PURGATORY

D uring the previous school year, I noticed that the principal of my daughter's school was starting to question her absences and chronic tardiness. As a teacher, I intimately knew what happens when a child is chronically absent and tardy.

The teacher will schedule a parent-teacher conference with you. If your child is still late or absent, you may get a call or a note from the principal. If changes still aren't made, your case will be brought up to the district level. The parents will be required to attend a meeting hosted by someone at the school district office. A sheriff deputy or truant officer will attend, along with an assistant superintendent and several other people.

Chances are pretty good that one of the other people to attend will be someone from Child Protective Services. They will explain your legal obligations as a parent to ensure the child attends school and is on time. Not ensuring your child gets an education is a form of neglect and abuse because every child in the United States is to be guaranteed an education. Getting to this point can take a few years.

In short, there is the possibility that the state could remove your child from your home. There are reasons for this protocol, and I know and understand that, having seen many situations first-hand.

We had a family meeting about the principal questioning my daughter's absences. The risk of telling any school official about our craziness is that our reality could have those officials seeing us as unfit parents. Did we want to take that risk? We did not and decided to have our daughter change schools for the upcoming fall school year.

The new school was a welcomed change for us and our daughter—a fresh start. Our daughter was excited to start over, and we were hoping that this change would also mean less paranormal activity. I don't know why we thought that would be the case because, in hindsight, it didn't make sense.

The first few weeks at her new school went well. She wasn't absent or tardy for almost three full weeks. And then it started to go downhill. The *Hat Man*, nicknamed Prissy, was back in her room staring at her day and night, the *three-headed crocodile* roaming the house, scaring the animals. There were so many other ghosts and negative beings roaming around, looking for help and trying to harass us. It felt like we were walking through sooty tar in our home.

It's kind of hard to describe, but when you have these low-frequency beings in your space all the time, your mind, body, and soul become fogged and in a depressed state. It was as if we were allowed to have a bit of a reprieve from the paranormal, and then it came barreling back at full speed.

I started getting emails from her teacher about the absences. I told her that my daughter had stomach issues.

That bought us some time. But as we were winding down for the Christmas break, things started ramping up again in a new and different way that I could have never predicted.

It was a Monday morning, and I entered my daughter's room to get her up for school. When I looked at her while she was sleeping, I noticed she had dark circles under her eyes and what looked like a bite mark on her neck by her clavicle. My heart sank.

I knew this meant she had a bad paranormal night, and she didn't wake me up. She dealt with it on her own. It's 6:30 am, and she has finally fallen asleep, and now I have to wake her up. She missed two days of school the prior week.

"I can't go to school," she said. "Something terrible will happen there, and I don't know what it is. Something terrible is going to happen."

"But you have to go, or we both might get in trouble," I told her.

Hearing that, she started crying. She was achingly tired, and now she has some type of fear that something terrible will happen at school. I asked her to tell me what she thought would happen.

"I don't know," she said. "Something really, really bad is going to happen. I don't know what it is."

And with that, we started our day, and she went to school with large dark circles of exhaustion under her eyes again. But nothing happened at school that day, for which I was thankful. However, her fears that something awful would happen at school escalated.

That night, while working on my computer, she came into my office to tell me that she thought that an evil man was going to come into the school with a gun.

"Why are you thinking this," I asked her, knowing that something was happening with her. This fear is not a part of her normal behavior.

"I don't know," she said. "I just keep getting a horrible feeling that a man is going to come to our school with a gun."

"Ok, if you get any other thoughts on this, let me know," I told her.

I was starting to wonder what was happening with my nine-year-old daughter. This wasn't like her at all. I decided to keep asking questions about it when she brought it up. I also decided that I would take notes to see if there were any clues or patterns that I could draw upon about this "man with a gun."

It was only Tuesday morning, but it felt like it should have been Friday at this point, as I had to get my exhausted kid up for school again. As I sat next to her bed, I could see she had tears streaming down her face. I was incredibly sad for her. She was living a nightmare she couldn't explain. That's the massive problem with paranormal influences. Many times, there are missing pieces to the puzzle, which makes it hard to determine what is happening.

## The Bad Man with the Gun Is Coming

"The bad man with a gun is coming to my school. He has one gun, but he has a lot more in his car," she said.

"What does he look like," I asked. "What color is his hair? How old do you think he is?"

She didn't know. Communicating what she was seeing, sensing, and feeling was so hard for her during this ordeal. I told her that was fair enough. As I dropped her off that morning, I felt so bad for her. She was exhausted and now filled with fear about some bad man coming to her school with a gun.

I have to admit, I was beginning to be alarmed as well. I wondered what was coming, if anything at all. Could this be a ghost haunting her that she couldn't fully see? If so, was it this ghost who killed people? Has this ghost killed children in the past? I was finally getting the hang of dealing with ghosts and crossing them over as best as possible. Or was it some type of dark entity who figured out a new way to torture us?

I had so many questions and so few answers.

"Mo-oooom!" she said, shaking me awake at the side of the bed. "Mom, I saw him!" she said.

It was almost four a.m. when she came into my bedroom. I got up, and we walked into her bedroom so that my husband could sleep for a bit longer before he had to get up and go to the office.

"Mom, I saw him in my dream," she said. "He has black hair. His head is shaped kind of weird, kind of like an upside-down eggplant. The top of his head is big, but the bottom half of his cheeks and mouth are kind of pointy. And mom, he has these weird, crazy eyes. He's coming to our school, and he's going to shoot the little kids! Mom, I'm so scared! I can't go to school." She started to cry.

I laid down with her in her bed and held her while she fell asleep. I just laid there wondering what all this meant. I let her sleep in that Wednesday morning, and she ended up sleeping until about noon and missing school that day.

Her poor, exhausted little body needed to rest more than she needed to sit in a chair and not have the energy to learn anything in school that day. She probably would have fallen asleep at her desk, and given that her teacher had a rather punitive personality type, that would not have been in her best interest. But then again, neither would a call from Child Protective Services be in her or our entire family's best interest.

What a fine line I was walking at that time.

She went to school very reluctantly on Thursday. I told her that I would volunteer in the break room making copies for teachers so that I would be on school grounds with her. I hoped that being near her would help to calm her down. And to be honest, I was getting somewhat worried about a man with a gun coming to the school.

There was nothing I could do about this. I couldn't go to the office or the principal and say, "You know, I think there may be a man coming to the school with a gun." First of all, I would have appeared crazy, and secondly, what could they do with that information? I didn't have a solid description or a name.

It was a long day for the both of us, but on the plus side, I got to take her home before the other parents clogged up the parking lot, and we didn't have to wait in a long traffic line.

It was one of those moments in time that I will never forget. It was near bedtime, and the girls were taking showers, getting ready for the next day. I was on my computer wrapping up some emails when my daughter came in, and these huge crocodile tears were just pouring down her face. She didn't say a word to me for the longest time. I just reached out and hugged and held her for a long time. I wasn't sure what was going on, but I suspected it was something about the man with a gun.

"Mom," she said softly. "I was in the bathroom brushing my teeth, and I saw him in the mirror. He's not old. He's white, has a weird-shaped head, and crazy eyes. He has on this heavy dark green vest, and he has a long gun. But there are more guns in his car. He's going to come to my school tomorrow. He's going to shoot the little kids! He's going to kill our principal, too! She's so nice. How can someone do that? He's a really angry man! My classroom is next to the little kids' classroom. He's going to kill them, Mom. I don't know what to do! I can't go to school tomorrow. But if I go, maybe I can save them. I'm so scared, mom. I don't know what to do." More tears gushed from her eyes as I continued to hold her.

I just hugged her and held her and asked her what seemed like a million questions, looking for a pattern or some insight, but I just couldn't come up with anything. She felt the need to go to school to warn others, but she also wanted to stay home.

"How about I drop you off in the morning, and I stay in the car and watch the parking lot for someone who fits the description of the bad man," I said. "I will keep the school and police numbers on my phone so I can call them fast to warn them if I see something. How does that sound to you?"

That night, I slept in her bed and held her while she slept. My mind was racing all night long. If I send her to school and there is a shooter, am I somehow knowingly putting my daughter in danger? If we don't go to school and there's a shooting, could we fail to help avert a tragedy? Was all this stuff about a bad man with a gun some premonition?

I felt like I was drowning. I only recently figured out how to cross over ghosts and send them to the higher realms. I was hoping this new skillset would lighten up that paranormal load we were dealing with, and *now this?*

I was starting to get angry. If this is a giant premonition, why would God send a prophetic image like this to an elementary-aged kid? This was one hell of a responsibility. But as angry as I was getting, I knew I had to focus on the present.

I stuck to my plan. I would take her to school and literally patrol the grounds with my cell phone in hand. I had no idea what would happen, but at least having some sort of plan felt helpful. I never said anything to my husband because I didn't know what this was or how to explain it to him fully, and he needed to focus on making a living on behalf of the family.

As the week went on, I wrote down everything my daughter was saying. I unwittingly wrote the playbook for a horrific tragedy yet to happen. Based on all our experiences with paranormal activity and how accurate my nine-year-old daughter was with her psychic ability, I was convinced that yes, indeed, an evil man with a gun would come to the school and he would kill a bunch of little kids, a teacher, and a principal. I was now convinced, as much as my daughter was, that he would come in with a long gun. Maybe a rifle. He had on a bulky dark green vest and drove a black car with the letter "H" on it.

As long as I live, I will never forget this Friday, December 14. It was a bright and sunny morning in Southern

California, and the air was crisp. This Friday was also only a few days away from my daughter's birthday. As I woke up my daughter on that fateful Friday morning, we both could feel the fatigue and terror. What was going to happen? At the same time, I was telling her - and myself - that nothing may happen.

As we got to the school, she looked at me and told me that if something happened, she couldn't call me from her cell phone because her teacher didn't allow them in the classroom. I told her to sneak it in this one time and put it in her pencil pouch.

She did not do that because her teacher watched her like a hawk that morning. Her teacher was angry that my daughter was absent one day this week and tardy on another day.

I held my daughter's face with both hands, told her I loved her, and kissed her goodbye. I reassured her that I would be in the parking lot where I could see her classroom. I promised her she was not alone. With that, she slipped out the car door, summoning all the nine-year-old courage and bravery she had in her, and walked into class.

I parked the car where I said I would and watched her classroom, looking for any man wearing a vest. I was also scanning the parking lot, and that is when I wondered if the letter "H" she saw meant "Honda." I turned on the radio in the car and just waited.

And then I heard it.

There was a school shooting in Connecticut. It was then that I realized the school shooter was not at her school but 3,000 miles away. I felt a massive sense of relief. Relief that my precious daughter and our school were safe.

At that exact moment, I felt a gigantic exhaling of breath that ousted all the tenseness and nerves I had been carrying this past week. My head plopped back into my seat. I smiled, then I wanted to cry but didn't. I knew my little girl, her friends, and her family would be safe.

They would all go home unharmed that night, unaware of a potential impending danger. But there was this other part of me that deeply grieved for all those parents and families who started their day just like any other day, and in a moment, their worlds were shattered. Those parents would never have that one last meal with their child, tuck them into bed, or remind them of a forgotten backpack. As I thought about those parents, I could only imagine how some would give anything to argue with their child about doing homework or chores around the house.

It was minutes before the school bell rang, and I jumped out of the car, pulled my daughter out of her room, and gave her a huge, long hug while I whispered in her ear that there was a school shooting and it was in another state and not her school.

At that moment, I dared not tell her about the children who were killed. The reports were still coming in, and the crime scene in this little town was still unfolding.

## Guilt and Grief of a Premonition

As we left her school that afternoon, she was full of questions. I told her let's get a snack and then talk about it. We arrived home, cut up some apples, and got out the peanut butter. She, her sisters, and I all ate at the table. It was at this moment I told them about the school shooting. The reports were still unfolding, but it was clear that this would grip the nation.

I shared with them what happened at this school and the level of devastation it had caused. We all cried at the table. The murdered kids and their families were probably no different than ours.

Up until then, the rest of my family didn't know what had been bothering her sister or me over that week. How could I have been sure until this moment? As a parent and spouse, it's tough to figure out what to share and not share with the rest of the family. I didn't want to keep secrets from them, but I needed to protect all my family in different ways. Would telling them have caused them increased anxiety? Would it have caused them to be fearful? What would the purpose of that be? What if we were wrong, and there was no shooting at all? As I was contemplating this event, my daughter started to sob at the table.

"I should have saved them, Mom," she said. "I should have done something to help them so this wouldn't have happened. This is all my fault. I knew there was going to be a shooting. Why, oh, why didn't I do something to stop this?"

I could barely make out her words as she was crying and practically hyperventilating.

And that's when her sisters intervened. They were trying to help her feel better by insisting there was nothing she could have done.

"If there was something you could have done, you know mom would have taken care of it," said one of her sisters. She believes in you, and we all do. You didn't know all the details. You thought this was your school. You didn't know this shooting would happen in another part of the country. In fact, we've never even been to Connecticut." Her sisters continued.

"You need to look at me right now," I said. "First, you are only nine years old. Second, for some reason, you had these premonitions. A premonition is the ability to see some future happening. *But* you were only given puzzle pieces. You were never given a location, the name of a school, or the name of the shooter. *Plus*, this happened 3,000 miles away from us. I want you to think about this for a moment," I firmly told her.

I know I was being a bit harsh, but I had to bring her back to reality. No amount of grief or guilt was going to fix this situation. No amount of grief or guilt was going to be helpful to her at all.

"Do you understand what I am telling you," I asked her.

"Yes, but it's tough," she said. "Seeing those kids all shot up is terrible."

"It's been a long week. Let's go lay down for a bit," I told her.

As I lay down with her, I could hear my other two girls watching a rerun of The Power Puff Girls. They were also on an emotional overload. I lay there just contemplating this entire scenario that unfolded this week.

Why *my* kid? I am just now getting the hang of crossing over ghosts. Annabelle and the little boy are now out of our home. Why did this premonition have to happen to her? I couldn't see any connection to figure out how my little girl saw this horrific event *before* it happened. After a while, I got up. I was doing some light cleaning and folding some laundry. For some reason, the typical day-to-day chores were a welcomed change of pace.

## The Letter

I went out to get the mail and found something that sank my heart. I found a letter from the school district sub-committee, SARC. This is an acronym for Student Attendance Review Committee. I knew what the contents of the letter would say, and after the week we just had, the week that culminated in me writing the playbook of one of the largest shooting massacres in the history of our country, which was dictated to me by my nine-year-old daughter.

I was emotionally drained. This was the one more thing that I could not handle at that moment. If there was ever the proverbial "straw that broke the camel's back," this was it. What an insanely long day to end an insanely long week, and now this.

The letter was addressed to my husband and me. It stated we must attend a meeting regarding our daughter's attendance and tardy issues in two weeks. As mad as I wanted to be at her teacher for raising this flag, as a teacher, too, I would have done the same. As mad as I wanted to be at her teacher, that would not be fair to me.

After all, her teacher had no idea that we had a three-headed crocodile roaming around the house scaring pets. She had no idea Prissy, the hat man, was constantly staring at us. This teacher had no idea that the ghost of a serial killer would come and go. This teacher had no idea that her student just had a premonition of epic horrors come to fruition.

If she had known about our family secret, she could have requested Child Protective Services to come and investigate. I get that. We had already changed schools this past year, hoping it would help our situation, but it didn't.

As heartbreaking as this letter was, it led us down another path. Sometimes, an opportunity can present itself in a new light in the darkest moments. Our daughter needed to thrive in the traditional public school system. We needed a solution that would better fit her needs, and we realized we needed to start looking into homeschool or charter school options.

If she had a tough night, there would be some flexibility in her day to sleep in late or even nap during regular school hours. The constant and chronic fatigue, stress, and horrors she was privy to needed balance. It was becoming evident that a traditional public school was unsuitable for a non-traditional life. Now, I had to add looking into alternative educational programs to my constant list of searching for paranormal guidance and help.

In the short term, we needed a plan to address this upcoming attendance (or lack of attendance) meeting. My husband and I talked about this letter all weekend whenever we could squeeze out a few private moments. We decided to gamble on our school principal.

This was a new school for us, and I didn't know her all that well. However, I did see that parents, students, and staff adored her. I would go in on Monday morning and request a meeting with her. It was risky, but the other option of burning the letter and pretending it didn't exist wouldn't solve this problem either.

The question now was, what do I do and say in this meeting? Can she even help us deflect this attendance review meeting? Does a principal have enough pull to make this go away? Then, it asks what we will do in the long term. We all wished this would stop. Whoever thinks these levels and varieties of psychic abilities are relaxed or fun has never walked in our shoes.

This school situation was not good. We also had another problem that was growing and looming in our home: dealing with the guilt and grief of a nine-year-old girl who was able to foresee one of America's most tragic mass murders.

Later that evening, my husband took our other two daughters out to a bookstore to give me and our little psychic some time alone. He and I both knew she needed some time to process these events. To make this more trying, as a parent, there are no parenting books, references, websites, or psychologists who could have helped us help her deal with this trauma.

Barely a minute after the rest of the family left the house, they all showed up. The scene unfolding in our living room was nothing I could have ever expected.

"I want my mommy! Where am I? I'm so scared. What happened? Why did that bad man shoot us?" The murdered little children were standing in my living room, crying. It looked like dozens. One boy had untied athletic shoes, another girl had bloodied long blonde hair, and another little girl wore an oversized dress. The screeching and crying reached a deafening pitch. My fragile nine-year-old girl cupped her hands over her ears as she squinted her eyes.

"Mom, the sound is hurting my ears," she said.

I could now also see their confusion. A look of shock, sadness, and fear appeared in their ghostly bodies, not knowing where they were located. Just minutes before, they felt the safety of their school; now, they landed in a strange place.

I was as speechless as they were homeless.

Just as my daughter and I felt hopeless in helping them, their principal suddenly appeared. My daughter described her as an adult with long brown hair dressed in business-like clothes. She acted like the leader she was in life, but now in death. Somehow, this principal managed to find and keep together all of her murdered students, and now some teachers appeared. These events were stunning as my daughter told me what was happening in the middle of our living room.

"Mom, the principal has quieted everyone down, and they are all sitting quietly," she said.

"Please ask the principal *how* she found us," I asked.

"She said that she found us through a bright light. She is also saying that she had to get all the children together before she could follow this light," my daughter said.

"The principal is furious that this happened," she said. "She is angry for the kids. She is saying that these children are also her children, and that this murderer should have never been allowed into the school. She's pissed, mom."

The word pissed is not something my daughter would say in front of me. Immediately, I felt the urge to cross over this group, but first, I had some questions I wanted to ask. I needed to know how this all worked. If this principal had some insight or knowledge to help me or my family, it would be helpful.

So many thoughts raced through my mind.

"Please tell the principal that we will help them all cross over and send them to a better place." Anxiously, I was hoping for some insights for us.

"How is it you were able to see this light that led you here?" I asked her.

"I was at the school, in a meeting, when we heard this popping noise," said the principal. "I had no idea what it was, and when I got up to investigate, that is when he shot me. I knew instantly I had died. Then I saw the light coming for me, but I couldn't go. I *had* to save my children. I knew there were a lot more victims. Once the shooting was over, it was weird. I was floating and calling out to anyone who could hear me to come to me.

"That's when the children started coming to me. I don't know how long it took, but I got them. At least, I think I got them all. God, I hope I got them all. I am thankful that the staff who were also murdered are with me. By the time I could get everyone, that light had vanished. I don't know why. I kept looking for the light and found the one that led me here. I don't understand where we are," the principal explained.

I told the principal that my daughter was having these premonitions about a school shooting, and maybe that is why they are here. I had no idea, but this made sense to me in this illogical dilemma. Or as much sense as I could make of the entire situation.

I also marveled at this principal's dedication to service. She was killed and saw this light to the Heavens come for her, and she chose not to go. In death, she used her free will to help her students and staff who were murdered by this same monster. Somehow, she could gather them all up and bring them here. I wish I knew how this worked.

I told my daughter to tell this group that we are bringing in teams of angels to help them cross over to Heaven to be with God right now. Sadly, all the children wanted us to give their parents, family, and friends messages. We explained to them that this was not something we could do, but once they crossed over, they could ask for help for their families.

With that, we could cross over this large group, and my daughter and I were grateful we could do this for them. My skills were growing, and this was one of the first larger groups that I helped cross over at the same time.

Based upon later news reports, we learned this horrific shooting occurred at Sandy Hook Elementary School in Connecticut. There were a total of 27 dead. Twenty were children. According to later reports, the others were staff, teachers, and the principal. The shooter committed suicide and was identified as a troubled youth with a history of mental illness.

My daughter slept and cried for most of that weekend. She couldn't stomach eating food. When the dreaded Monday came upon us, she still looked exhausted. The constant dark circles under her eyes were even darker.

I decided to let her miss another day of school. I wondered, what the heck, what's another day? Plus, it was her birthday, and she was so tired she didn't even remember it. My greatest birthday wish for my child was that someday she could have a normal and happy birthday with friends, presents, and a cake.

I decided to drive to the school alone and walked into the office, where I saw the school nurse and explained that my daughter was absent for the day. She rolled her eyes at me as if I could hear her think, "Absent again."

I then asked the secretary to make an appointment with the principal as soon as possible. Her earliest opening was after school that same day. "Even though you aren't picking up your daughter today, could you please return at 3:45?" the secretary asked me.

I told her yes and thanked her for her time.

I was nervous all day long. This was a gamble, and I had hoped the bet would pay off. I remembered telling the 'higher powers that be' and God they needed to help me with this meeting. I needed help explaining to the school officials to understand our living nightmare.

I was acutely aware of the delicate balance between them being freaked out, calling Child Protective Services, and believing my story. First, attendance has never been an issue with my other children; second, I was a teacher in this school district; and third, I understand the importance of attending school and being on time.

It was then that I realized I needed to come to this meeting armed. I gathered up my "playbook" of the recent school shooting that I inadvertently wrote and the letter from the district. My stomach was in knots all day, and it got worse as I drove to the school for this meeting. This meeting was so important that it could dictate what would happen with our family, for better or worse.

I got out of my car and walked into the office, where I was greeted by the secretary, who, ironically, was a former neighbor. Sometimes, it is a small world. She led me into the conference room, where I saw the principal and my daughter's teacher.

I remember thinking, "Great". This teacher already doesn't like my kid, and I get it. When a student is absent and tardy, it creates extra work like homework packets and making up missed tests and quizzes, which is just the beginning. I took a deep breath and sat down.

## The Meeting

As I started talking, this calm came over me, and I swear the words coming out of my mouth weren't mine. Maybe my prayers were answered after all.

"We all have heard the word 'ghost' before, and I need to share some personal insights about my daughter," I said. "She can see and hear entities and ghosts, which has been difficult for her and us. They come at her at night and day, and we are struggling with this as a family. It's tough on her. She wants a break."

I stopped talking and waited for a reaction. Should I explain more? Should I tell them about my psychic ability? It felt like an eternity was passing by at a glacial pace, waiting for one of them to speak.

The principal looked at me with surprisingly sympathetic eyes, and I wasn't sure how to read her. She reached her hand out and put it on top of my hand. I was shocked. I did not anticipate that.

"I do understand," the principal told me. "I am rather spiritual and think I know what you mean."

The teacher didn't say a word, and I was somewhat dumbfounded. Then, all of a sudden, my stomach, which was full of knots, started to relax fully.

"I want to show you something." As I slid a notebook across the table to her.

"This is what we dealt with all last week," I said. "These are the notes I was taking as my daughter was dictating to me why she was scared to come to school last week. This notebook is full of the premonitions *my* daughter had about the recent school massacre. Only she thought that it was *her* school where the tragedy would happen. I wrote down everything she said about it as she was 'seeing' this tragedy."

Sitting across the table from the Principal, I reflected on how difficult these episodes have been for me as a parent and my family over the past three years. Next came a surprising emotional outburst. As hard as I tried, I couldn't hold back the tears, and by now, I had gotten quite good at holding things in, not revealing my true feelings.

I took a deep breath and steadied my voice. "How do I make sure my daughter is safe?" I continued to explain. "How do I teach her that the guilt she is feeling over these deaths is *not* her fault? No one outside our family knows of the hell we have been living in, and now I get this letter from SARC. I don't know what to do. I know that next year, we will enroll her in a home or charter school so she can learn on her own terms. I am a certified teacher, and I know what to do."

When I finished, a steady stream of tears rolled down my face, and I simply sat there, not saying a word or uttering any sound. I was frozen in my chair, watching the principal read the letter.

"I will make this go away," said the principal. "Try to get your daughter to school as much as possible, and your choice to home-school her is in her best interest."

I thanked them as we all left the conference room.

I have yet to receive another letter from SARC again, and the following school year, we began homeschooling.

I will never forget this principal. Her ability to understand what we were going through and to quietly make this go away gave me hope that we did have some spiritual team looking out for us. I say this because there were many times when I questioned whether any of this was real. Looking back, karma was in play. I had two extraordinary experiences with two remarkable principals in two different dimensions.

Thankfully, my daughter has not had any more premonitions quite like that. I realized these premonitions happened because my daughter was somehow in resonance with those schoolchildren who were 3,000 miles away. Could these two principals also have been in resonance with one another due to their sense of dedication to their students?

This experience also made me realize that we all have limitless potential futures with each choice we make. Perhaps some futures are set in stone for some reason.

Could this massacre have been one of them? Could my daughter have these suspicions so we could help this group of souls to cross over? What would have happened to them if they had not connected to my daughter? Would they still be in a ghostly limbo? Would they have followed in Annabelle's footsteps? Ghost children looking for their parents?

I don't know the answers, and I still have many questions. I understand that every experience we have will teach us lessons for our soul's karmic path, and this one was a doozy. I am very grateful that we were able to help them all cross over.

# GUILT AND FLAILING BULLETS

The unexpected death of a child or teenager sends shock waves through all parents. This type of story happens every day across the United States. Every city and town has had to live with a sudden death in their community.

You don't even have to know the victims personally, and yet, somehow, you still feel it. That sad, melancholy feeling of how fragile life can be stuck to our senses while feeling the need to hug your kids a little tighter, to tell them that you love them—the desire to call or text your friends to say hello and reconnect with their mounts.

Around 8:30 pm, I was folding laundry again in my bedroom when my daughter casually walked in with a newspaper. She opened it up to the front page, but I already knew what she would show me and tell me. I could feel them coming.

"Mom, this boy is standing next to me, and he says he needs help," said my daughter. "He says his name is Lucas, and this is him. He has a bullet hole in his forehead, pointing at the front headline of the local paper.

It struck me as odd but, sadly, normal. The way my little girl, so matter of fact and without fear or drama, told me that this dead teen was standing next to her illustrated how much death and sadness she has been witness to these past couple of years.

There was also a shift in me. My surprise about hearing these events waned. My emotional reaction felt dulled. Was it because I was beginning to understand more about how the spiritual world works? I just listened.

I asked him how he had found us. He said he had just seen a bright light, followed it, and ended up in our home. We keep hearing from the dead that our house is a beacon of bright light. I'm not sure if it is the house or the people who are creating this bright light.

He went on to say that this is the warmest he has felt since his death. He also said that he finally felt safe once he entered our home. He said that all these dark, shadowy beings have been constantly harassing him, and it has been terrifying for him, to put it mildly.

"Lucas, what do you want to tell us?" I asked.

At this point in our paranormal journey, I can better see beings and sense abnormal vibrations. My abilities were growing more robust, which was a relief as it took pressure off my daughter.

Lucas began his sad story, which captivated me. "I know my parents didn't know I was doing drugs, and I realize now that I was doing more than I should have been," said Lucas. "I feel awful about this, and I want my parents to know that this wasn't their fault. Can you please tell my mom to stop blaming herself?

"She keeps saying that she knew I was on drugs and that she could have stopped me. This is not her fault because I was good at hiding it. I feel so bad I caused my family so much pain. I don't know what to do," Lucas said.

I sensed a mounting discomfort in Lucas and asked him if he was worried about his mom.

## Please Talk to My Mom

"Yes! Please tell her not to hurt herself," he said. "She is taking a lot of pills right now to make her not get depressed. I am worried she will take too many and end up hurting herself. My brother still needs a mom. It's bad enough he's now an only child because I was too stupid to do the right thing. Please tell her she can talk to my dad about this stuff. She doesn't need to keep her pain from him. I'm so worried about my family and what I did to them because I was stupid," he said.

Regret filled him as he talked about the behavior that led to his death.

Poor Lucas was now crying and sobbing uncontrollably, and my laundry still wasn't folded. But in all seriousness, the dead can grieve more than most may ever realize. This poor kid is learning how his careless actions echo out to those he loves and cares about.

We just let him talk. I took notes, looking for clues.

"Tell Derek," He sobbed. "Please tell Derek I should have been looking out for him more. He was the only friend that I had whom I cared about. He was always trying to straighten me out. He was my only friend who was not doing drugs! Can you believe that? Drugs are everywhere, and they are so regular and accessible. Why? Why is that?

"My dad needs to know that even though we didn't have the best relationship, I have always loved him and still love him. And you need to tell my parents they shouldn't do it," he said.

"Do what?" I asked him through my daughter.

"The lawsuit," he replied. "They shouldn't do the lawsuit because this was all my fault. I was the one who brought the drugs in. I snuck them into the house. It was me. It was all my fault. It was not my friends' fault. I did it. I bought them in downtown San Diego one night when my parents were asleep."

"What exactly did you buy?" I asked him.

"I bought marijuana that was laced," he said. "It had something different in it, something special. I bought it so my buddies and I could have fun when our parents left for dinner that night.

"Our three families have been friends for a long time, and we boys always hung out. I got this special pot for us. It was expensive, but it was supposed to be amazing. I could have never imagined what would end up happening. We think we're all invincible. That nothing can hurt us. That's the problem with teens and drugs," he said.

Lucas began to tell in detail the actions that led up to his death. "That night, when our parents left, we started a campfire in the backyard, and that is when I pulled out this special bag. I was so excited to share this with them. I know it sounds stupid now, but I didn't know. We started smoking the pot, and all of a sudden, we could all see these black, swirling, shadowy things coming at us. It freaked us out.

"We ran all over the backyard to escape them, but more kept showing up. It was horrible! They were so scary flying around with their red beady eyes. There must have been hundreds of them! That's when we thought they would go away if we could shoot at them," he said.

"I went into the house to get my dad's black pistol, which was on the countertop in the kitchen," he said. "He had just bought it. It was his pride and joy. Earlier in the day, he was shooting cans with it in the backyard.

These black things followed me into the house when I entered the kitchen. Then they started to fill up the house, too. What did I do? What are these things? Where did they come from?" He asked as terror filled his voice.

I asked who shot him.

"It doesn't matter who shot me," he said. "It doesn't matter because I was the one who did all of this. This is my fault. This is ALL my fault. I was the one who got my friends to do drugs. If it weren't for me, they may have never started doing drugs.

"If I had done things differently, I'd still be alive, and my family would still be friends with the other families. It was all fun and games until it wasn't. And now my friends might go to jail because of what I did to them. Oh, God, I feel so bad." He was sobbing.

"In the next moment, I realized I was not in my body anymore." he said." I was watching the police and paramedics. They didn't even try to revive me. They just covered me up and took away my body. I must have been dead."

"It was like watching a movie as I panned towards my parents and our friends. They were all sobbing and in disbelief. How could I have done this to them? This is all my fault, and now my parents want to put my friends in jail for something I did. I don't know what to do. These shadowy beasts are still following me around and still in my house!" Lucas said.

All the while my daughter and I were listening to his story, I had to marvel at how wise and calm she appeared. She never lost sight of her goal to help this poor kid in the same grade as one of her sisters. It all hit so close to home. Lucas could be any parent's child.

Lucas wanted me to relay these messages to his friends and family. This concept had several problems, such as the fact that it looks great on TV but doesn't work in real life.

The first problem is that I don't know his parents or friends. Even though I don't know them, I know that they are probably still grieving. I don't know their personal beliefs. Do they believe in an afterlife? Do they believe in ghosts and these other entities that latched onto these boys?

I had to tell him that as much as I wanted to share what he told us with his family and friends, I couldn't do that as it would be even more upsetting to them.

I explained that once he crosses over, there will be Divine beings there to help him. They will help him with his grief, help him to heal, and better understand this life just lived. Once there, I told him he could ask for help with healing for his family and friends.

He told us he didn't deserve to go to Heaven. I told him he doesn't deserve to be in limbo as a ghost. He just went through a massive trauma. There is no judgment.

When I crossed him over, he thanked us for our time and help. He was always so kind and polite, and he was ready to go.

# HE OUTLIVED SUPERMAN

Tom was a family friend, an extraordinarily nice guy. So was his family. He worked hard all his life, and he was always willing to help out a fellow friend, neighbor, or family member. He's the kind of guy who would give you the shirt off his back if you needed it. We all know of a person like this and wish we knew more people like him. If more Toms existed, our world would be a better place.

I had a flashback in time. It was a typical Saturday afternoon in my southwestern Michigan neighborhood. Spring had finally arrived, removing the gray chroma that would permeate the buildings and vegetation. Even the color of people's faces brightened with spring blossoms and green foliage. The changing of seasons is a fond memory from my childhood. It was the time of year when you could feel the new energy moving in. This also meant it was time for spring cleaning, gardening, and planting.

Farmers in outlying areas had been disking their fields for weeks, preparing for spring corn planting. Our family friend, Tom, was a generational farmer who took over from his father the duties associated with the family farm. He loved it.

He loved his tractors. He loved fixing them, and he loved the smell of the fresh, rich soil as he turned it over.

One day, Tom ventured out to the far end of the farm, which encompassed hundreds of acres. Most often, his wife, Mary, packed him lunch because the trek back to the house took away the valuable time he could spend disking his fields. Many times, Mary would not see her husband until dinner time.

But on this fateful day, Mary would be waiting for Tom long past his normal return home time. As Tom was driving his John Deere 4450 along an irrigation ditch, the right side of a disk roller caught hold of a downed tree limb, which stopped the gear mechanism.

Upon hearing a clanking noise, Tom immediately stopped the tractor and took it out of gear; with the tractor engine still running, he walked back to take a look. Unable to lodge loose the tree limb, he climbed aboard the tractor to reverse it. As he climbed aboard, his hand grabbed the steering wheel. His foot slipped from the mud on the sole of his boot. He accidentally grabbed the gear shift.

That motion thrust the tractor forward, simultaneously knocking Tom to the ground. The dual tires ran across the midsection of his body while he lay face down. Suddenly, for whatever reason, the tractor stopped on top of Tom. He was stuck, unable to move. He started to yell, although, being miles away from the house and barn, he realized no one could hear him.

He lay squished with a four-ton, 200-horsepower John Deere tractor on his back.

Mary became concerned when Tom failed to return home for dinner that evening. She called a mutual family friend who lived nearby, and they drove to where he was working and found Tom. He lay lifeless, unconscious but breathing. The friend called for help as Mary kneeled beside her husband, sobbing.

This accident changed his life, his family's life, and our friendly community forever.

## The Accident

He was transported by ambulance to the hospital. Later, family and friends were told he would be paralyzed and in a wheelchair for the rest of his life. Quadriplegic.

People were in shock, including me. I liked Tom. As it turned out, he stayed in a wheelchair for the rest of his life with a spinal injury, leaving paralysis in his arms and legs. The accident left everyone wondering why bad things happen to good people. Tom was an upstanding guy, and so were his wife and kids. So many of us, including me, struggled searching for the answers as to why this terrible freak accident happened to such a beloved man. In a single flash, in a single act in time, his world would never be the same.

It was months before Tom could return to his home from the hospital. As tragic as this was, karma was not wasting energy on Tom or his family. Everyone stepped in to help Tom and his wife and two young kids. Meanwhile, everyone pitched in to make his home wheelchair accessible by building a ramp to the front door and clearing pathways. The neighbors pitched in with the usual farm chores Mary could not do herself. The vegetables in their garden came on while Tom was in the hospital. We all helped Mary pick cucumbers and green beans.

Their friends patiently ensured the family had everything they needed during those exceptionally trying times.

Shortly after Tom's accident, the movie actor Christopher Reeves, suffered the same paralyzing spinal injury as Tom. The good news was that since Reeves was famous and wealthy, it focused on spinal cord injuries and new research in this area. Christopher Reeves and his wife devoted their time, money, and energy to working with leading doctors and scientists.

The media attention and publicity from Reeve's injury gave Tom, his family, and our community renewed hope. Because of Christopher Reeves, many new therapies for spinal cord damage were explored. National attention was gained for injuries that were once previously ignored. An expectation existed that maybe some regenerative treatment could be made available to help Tom.

The coincidences in time and severity of Tom's and Chris' injuries were not lost on me.

Sadly, Christopher Reeves finally succumbed to pneumonia and died. When Tom heard this news, he was devastated, and so was his family and our community. We all likened Superman's life to our friend Tom.

During his years as a quadriplegic, Tom never gave up. He never retreated. He spent years as a volunteer tutoring school-aged kids, teaching young farmers how to maintain their equipment, and passing on historical accounts of farming through storytelling. It was clear that nothing slowed down Tom. This man had survived incredible odds and never, ever wasted a day. He never, ever wavered in his faith in God, nor did his family.

Fast forward over 20 years later, I received a call from an old neighbor friend about Tom. She told me that he had been hospitalized and died suddenly. I hung up the phone and started making dinner. The house began to quiet down as the evening progressed with our normal homework activities and cleaning the dinner dishes. I started thinking about Tom.

Indeed, Tom would cross over. He was a wise soul who never questioned his faith in God and was an exceptional person. He also knew that death was inevitable.

I was in my bedroom folding laundry yet again. Looking back, I think I have logged more hours as a mom folding laundry than anything else. I had three kids in sports, and that created constant piles of laundry. As I was folding that laundry, I started thinking about Tom. I now realize that when a person dies, they leave their mortal body and can travel at the speed of thought.

In an instant, Tom appeared in my bedroom. I was a bit startled but not completely surprised, as I was always in communication with his son and daughter.

"Tom, why are you here? Why didn't you go into the light?" I asked. If anyone were to die and cross over, it surely would be Tom. I mean, this guy is a fantastic soul in so many ways.

His response stunned me. It's something I will never forget.

## A Human Mind Construct Conundrum

"I know I died. I can still see the light, but I don't know *how* to get there," said Tom. "I have no one to assist me in going to the light. I haven't been able to walk or use my arms for over 20 years. When I died, I was in bed and not in my wheelchair.

How can I possibly go into the light without assistance? I am
not sure what to do to get there."

This was a huge ah-ha moment for me.

Tom was so used to not being mobile that he relied on the
assistance of others so much that when the light came for him,
he felt utterly helpless. This was such a massive revelation for
me. He was so used to having people do everything for him
that when the light came, he just stood there. He did not realize that he could now move himself.

"How is it that I am here, in your house, and how can you
talk to me?" Tom was clearly confused as he drilled me for
answers. "No one else can talk to me. I'm watching my family
crying, crying tears of sadness and joy simultaneously. The
freedom is amazing! How did I get here?" he asked.

"Tom, I was simply thinking about you, and you popped
in here for some reason. I think I can help you. I have an odd
question to ask you, though. I'm curious: can you feel your
arms and legs?" I asked.

"No, I can't," he said.

"Hmmmm. I want to request that an angel come into this
room to help you restore the feeling in your arms and legs.
Would that be okay with you?"

Even though Tom was now a ghost, I felt it was important
to ask him for permission. I didn't want to violate his free
will. I had no idea if he would be open to this concept. I also
had no idea if it would work. After all, I had never encountered a paralyzed ghost before.

"Sure. I still can't believe I'm here," said Tom. "I have to
be honest. I am glad that I finally left my broken body, but
at the same time, that fractured body gave me more time to

spend with my wife and family. If you can, please tell my wife that I am grateful for all of the years of loyalty and service she gave me. She is a wonderful wife, and I say IS, and not WAS, for a reason.

"She is a wonderful wife. Please tell her I am eternally grateful for her years of love and support. She took the 'in sickness and in health' part of our marriage vows seriously. She never once wavered. I don't believe there is any wife better than my wife. I don't know what I did to deserve all those years of unconditional love and support she gave me. It was hard for her to take me places, but I loved getting out and helping people. She will always be my world," he said.

His comments melted my heart. This family went through a life-changing event. I requested an angel who could help heal Tom. Immediately, he arrived and was about six feet tall. I could see him infusing Tom with some sort of light-glowing substance. It was a fantastic technique to watch. His whole body, arms, and legs were glowing and pulsating as the angels worked on him.

"How are your arms and legs feeling? I requested angels to help with healing and restoration," I told him.

"Wow. I am feeling numbness and tingling all over, and I can move my arms! Oh. My. Goodness! I. . . I don't know what to say other than thank you!" he said.

"You can thank the angels for helping you with this. I honestly wasn't sure if this would work or not. I just trusted my intuition on this one," I told him.

Just then, one of my daughters walked into the room, ready to help me with this pile of laundry. She could also see what was happening.

"Who's here," she asked me.

"This is one of Grandpa Russ' friends. He died recently, and he came here," I told her.

"You have children," he asked. "Did you know I have grandchildren? I have three. Two girls and a boy! They are so much fun to watch. My daughter would bring them down every other weekend. The youngest just learned how to ride a bike. I would have my wife take me outside, and I would race them down the street or down the long driveway in my wheelchair. It was so much fun just listening to them all laugh and squeal in delight as they would beat me in the race. I'm going to miss that.

"Wow! Can you and your daughter also see and talk to me? This is incredible. I had no idea you could do these things. How is your dad? I know he died, but do you know how he's doing? Do you get to talk to him now that he is gone, too? I have so many questions." Tom rattled off questions faster than I could answer.

"Well, that's a long story," I said. "But the short answer is he is now in Heaven, so he doesn't visit us as a ghost anymore. We all miss him, but we understand that he has other jobs he is doing now. We also understand that love never dies. It transcends dimensions. By the way, how are your arms and legs feeling? I am inquisitive about all of this."

"I just realized I can now move my arms and legs! Wow! What a joyous moment. I forgot what this felt like. Thank you," he said.

"No need to thank me," I said. "It's the angels doing this work. I admit I am not sure what the angels are doing, but it's cool to watch. I can see all these brilliant colors being infused into your soul essence.

"I think it's time to cross you over so you can go Home. You have lived such an extraordinary life of love, faith, kindness, and compassion. It's an honor to know you. I will request this angel to help your crossover right now," I told him.

"Thank you," he said. "I can't believe I get to do this. I can't believe my arms and legs work again. Do you think I can eat roast beef up there? That's my favorite food,"

"I don't know, but it can't hurt to ask. I am requesting an angelic escort for you right now," I told him.

That's when two more angels and another being showed up in my bedroom. I was stunned when I realized who this third entity was, and so was my daughter. It was my dad! My dad somehow was able to present himself to us! It was so good to see him. Yet, I couldn't figure out why he was there. Once a soul crosses over into Heaven, they generally aren't allowed to come back until their next incarnation. But here was my dad, sandwiched between two angels. They both nodded to my dad, and that is when he spoke.

"You're welcome for the car parts," my dad told Tom as they laughed. I had no idea what that was all about.

I guess humor does transcend realms.

"Did you know your daughter and granddaughter could do these kinds of wonders," Tom asked my dad.

"Yes," said my dad. "I am so glad you found them. I came here to assist you to cross over into Heaven. You're going to love it here," he told Tom.

"Do I get to eat roast beef? I would love to be able to feed myself for a change," he full-heartedly laughed.

"Come on, Tom. Let's go," said Dad. Tom and my dad were sandwiched between the three angels walking away, up towards a beam of light, when my dad turned around momentarily and gave me the biggest smile.

Love never dies. It merely transcends dimensions.

# AN UNUSUAL HIGH SCHOOL
# REUNION

"**M**om, a ghost here says she knows you." My daughter told me. "She says her name is Emily, and she is asking if she can babysit me. It looks like she was in an accident or something. Her head is banged up pretty bad."

A flood of memories instantaneously hit me. Emily? Here? Right now? Emily was one of my closest childhood friends. Growing up in southwest Michigan, we lived on different lakes. But the two lakes were connected. A small tunnel connected the lakes below, and above it was a two-car road. We would each canoe over to the tunnel from our respective lakes and meet in the middle. During the warm weather months, we often ate lunch while seated in our canoes anchored in shallow water.

In the winter, we would go sledding in the hills behind our houses until dark. One winter, when I was ten, I crashed my sled into a tree at the bottom of the hill and broke my foot. Emily ran a quarter mile back to my house to get my dad. While Dad carried me up the hill in the deep snow, Emily was at my side, worrying the whole way home.

Some of my best childhood memories involved Emily.

Her death was an anchor point in time for me. To this day, I can recall with vivid detail that fateful phone call when I first learned of my dear friend's death. As young adults, we tend to think we are invincible, and when the unimaginable happens, a new reality sets in that permeates our souls. It makes you grow up fast. It makes you realize our impact within our circles of family and friends.

While home from my second year in college on Christmas break, I was in my brother's bedroom talking to him when the phone rang. I remember all the details of his room at that moment. The pile of clothes was on the floor, one of the closet doors was open, and there was a hole in the screen from when he decided to shoot a bottle rocket from his room.

It was as if time stretched out before me.

My mom answered the phone and told me the call was for me. I picked up the phone that was in my brother's room. It was my friend, Mik. I always looked forward to hearing from Mik and anticipated her asking me to go to the mall or some other fun event with her. This time, her voice sounded funny. At first, I thought she was giggling, but then I realized she was holding back tears.

"Em. . . Emily. . . died. Emily is gone. The car she was in hit black ice and crashed." Mik told me.

Back in my room with my daughter, I remembered being silent. I instantly relived moments with Emily from all those years ago as I leaned against my bed, pondering a load of unfolded laundry. I then pulled myself back to my current reality.

As I thought back, not only was I looking forward to being home for Christmas with family and friends, but Emily's birthday was just two days away. She would never see 20.

Instantly, another wave came over me when I thought about her twin brother Eli. He would suffer through their shared birthday all alone for the first time in his life and for the rest of his life.

My daughter had no idea how important this person was to me. "Hold on a moment," I told my daughter while trying to compose myself.

Turning to my daughter, I began to explain. "Emily was one of my childhood friends who died in a car accident one winter night. I need a minute to process this, and I have many questions I would like to ask her."

"Can you help me with Emily? I don't think I can do it myself. How about I take you shopping for a thank-you gift when we're done." I told her. I didn't offer to take her out as a bribe, but I felt it was important to respect her abilities and not to take advantage of what she could do.

This was a bit emotional for me, and emotions can cloud psychic hearing.

## I Needed Help

I knew I needed her help because I was in shock. We had been dealing with paranormal phenomena for quite a while, and by now, I have learned how to cross over lost souls. How could I have missed my dear childhood friend? How is it that I never thought to 'look' for her? What kind of a friend did that make me?

I was starting to feel guilty about all of this. But I quickly realized I had a job to do. Any potential guilt that was beginning to well up inside me served no purpose, and I had to let it go.

It would have been easy to simply cross Emily over, as I have done dozens of times before with lost and lonely souls. Both love and loss flooded me. I wanted to take a few minutes to talk with my old friend. As selfish as that may have seemed, I wanted to hear from her one last time. I still missed her. It never occurred to me that she had not crossed over until now, and I inadvertently felt responsible.

"Ok. I'll translate for you." My daughter was eager to help.

Emily started talking through my daughter, "I didn't know you had kids. I haven't seen you in so long," said Emily. "I would love to babysit your daughters." Emily was wearing a light blue sweater scattered with snowflakes and a winter coat, which I recognized.

It was then I realized the problem. My friend had no idea she died over 20 years ago.

My heart went out to her. My sadness deepened even further, remembering she had such a hard life growing up. Now, in death, it seemed her lousy luck followed her. She was stuck in a dimension she didn't know or understand.

I was curious as to how this affected her. I also knew that I needed to break the news to her that she had died, and that was going to be a harsh blow.

"Emily, do you know that you died," I asked her.

Silence overtook her. It was as if she needed ghostly time to process this information. As she was standing in my bedroom, I asked for an angel to come and be with her. I had learned the importance of angels as comfort for both the living and the dead.

"Wow. This makes a lot of sense," said Emily. "I couldn't understand why my mom and siblings wouldn't talk to me. I would get so angry at them for ignoring me all the time. I felt like they didn't care about me at all. And then, one day, they left the house, and all of these new people arrived. I finally found my brother again and realized he got married! Now I know why he didn't tell me. When I tried to visit my friends from college, no one would ever talk to me. I felt so invisible, so alone. For a long time, I could see people crying, and I didn't know why they were crying."

I often felt emotions from the spirits or souls we crossed over, yet I was able to detach myself somewhat from them. However, with my dearest friend Emily, my emotional status was raw, real, and so exposed. In an altering moment, I realized that ghosts have the same emotions as people. Just because our physical bodies die doesn't mean our feelings die.

"Was it because I died?" Emily asked. "I guess they do love me. I thought that no one loved me since everyone was always ignoring me." She started to cry.

"Emily, I wish I could hug you, but you do need to know that you were and are loved very much," I told her. "I think what happened is that when you were suddenly ejected out of your body, you had no concept that you had died.

"One moment, you are a passenger in a car, and the next moment, the car you were in hit black ice and slid off the road, hitting two trees and a parked semi-truck. It all happened so fast. We were all so devastated. You have no idea," I explained.

I have learned that the dead can hear us when we talk to them; I just had to work on the listening part so I could listen to them better. I could see she felt better about the unintentional neglect she had endured from all her beloved people still on earth.

It was just one of those bad situations. But I was so relieved that she found me. We talked a bit more, and she was feeling better and better. I told her it was time to cross her over so she could finally go Home.

I requested an angel to cross her over. He looked at us and raised his hand with palm upward, indicating to wait. That's when my daughter and I both saw a second angel accompanied by Emily's father, who died when she was 13 years old.

I was stunned.

That type of event doesn't usually happen. Emily's dad thanked us for helping his daughter finally come home. He said he had been waiting a long time to be able to bring her Home, as he was hugging her for dear life. When we finished talking, her father grabbed her by the hand, and the angels escorted them to Heaven.

I've seen this many times when a circle of white light opens up, and those angelic beings cross over the souls who need help. It's quite a humbling experience and quite an honor. I used to be so angry that all of these souls would invade my home, and I didn't know what to do about it. Now that I have learned how to be of assistance, I look at this as part of my mission.

I went to bed that night with my mind reeling. I wanted to share this with my friends and Emily's family. This paranormal lifestyle was still a big secret in our family. At the time, maybe five outsiders knew about this at most. If I were to tell anyone, I honestly don't know how it would be received. It's not like this is a made-for-TV movie where everything works out in the end. This is real life. This is a real-life trauma. This is real death. The trauma continues to echo out whether we are aware of it or not.

The spiritual realm has so much influence over the physical worldly realm, manifesting in ways we often fail to understand. Most of us assume that when a person dies, they automatically cross over into Heaven. Many, like Emily, who are suddenly ejected out of their bodies in an accident or natural disaster, have no idea they died. Then, they become stuck as ghosts. They are stuck between Heaven and Earth until some event happens where they can get assistance. If that assistance ever comes.

We all suffered a massive loss with Emily's death. I decided not to say anything to anybody for now. The important message for me was that my friend could finally cross over and go Home. Knowing she was now in God's hands made me feel better.

Just when I assumed that all was well with Emily, a month later, I got an announcement about a high school reunion coming up, and it had me thinking of Emily and her twin brother, Eli, again. I shared this with a friend. I wanted his advice. Do I say anything or not?

He recommended that I talk to an old family friend about this. A dear woman named Melanie, whom I regarded as my second mom, knew Emily. More importantly, she understood the paranormal world. I thought this was a great idea and would call her the next day.

"Hi, Melanie," I said.

"Hi honey, how are you? I miss you so much," she instantly recognized my voice. To this day, hearing her voice still makes me a bit homesick.

"I'm good, and so is my family. Um, listen, I want to share an event with you, and I need confidentiality. This is huge, and I am not sure what to do about this situation, if anything at all," I told her.

"Of course. What's going on?" she asked me.

"Emily showed up at my house last month," I told her.

"EMILY?" she exclaimed.

"Yes. Here's the situation," I said. "She had no idea she had died. She couldn't understand why no one would speak to her or answer questions. But I was able to help her understand what happened. We crossed her over, and her dad showed up with an angelic escort. It was incredible. But here's my dilemma: do I share this with her brother? Or do I let it go? Do you know how Eli feels about these happenings?"

"I don't know, but I'm attending a luncheon tomorrow," said Melanie. "Eli's wife, Veronica, will be there. What timing. I can be discreet and try to understand how she feels about this situation."

The next day, Melanie called me back.

"I had a great lunch with Veronica," Melanie said. "She told me that they do believe in the presence of ghosts. She wants to know if they can call you. It was tough not to spill the beans. I hope you don't mind, but I gave them your number, and they will probably call you today," she said.

I thanked her for her help. I was so excited to talk with Eli and Veronica, friends whom I hadn't seen in 20 years since I moved to California.

Not one minute passed when Melanie hung up, and Eli, Emily's twin brother, called me.

## Her Twin Brother

"Hello?" he said somewhat hesitantly.

"Eli?" I asked.

"Yes, I hear you have a story for me," said Eli. "Veronica met Melanie and a bunch of other women for a luncheon, and they got to talking. I am dying to hear what happened. Something also happened to me, and now I think it makes sense. But you tell me first."

"Well, where do I start? I am no longer a schoolteacher anymore," I said. "Our family life took a hard-left turn into the paranormal a couple of years ago, and it has been quite a ride. Anyway, about a month ago, Emily showed up at my house, and I was stunned. It was great to speak with her. She had no idea she had died. She wanted to babysit my girls. We ended up crossing her over, and in the process, your dad came to meet her, and together, they crossed her over into Heaven. It was truly amazing and unforgettable."

"Wow, I am so relieved," said Eli. "It's been almost five weeks since I felt this shift – it was immediate and amazing. I can't even begin to describe how the weight of the world has been lifted from my shoulders. Everything seems lighter now. I don't know how else to describe it. I am finally free, but I am unsure what I am free from. Does this make sense?"

Ever since Emily's death, Eli told me he dealt with a type of depression, and he could never figure out why. He felt like his sister was with him a lot of the time. But that was normal because don't our departed loved ones watch over us? Eli also shared with me that he had an argument with Emily before the accident. I suspect a part of the depression could have been a form of guilt he may have felt.

That argument was the last time they spoke. It affected him, as it would with anybody. It got me thinking that it's simply a part of human nature to argue or conflict with our loved ones, especially family. But just because we have a disagreement doesn't mean that we don't love them. It's the opposite. Plus, Emily never remembered they had a disagreement.

When Eli told me he somehow felt lighter, it said to me that his depression may not have been his. It was more probable that the depression was his sister's. She didn't realize that she had died, and everyone was always ignoring her. She felt isolated and alone by no fault of anyone. It was just a bad set of circumstances. The energy of her grief and despair overshadowed Eli. It's a type of energy that we can't usually see nor readily understand.

She didn't understand she had died. As a ghost, she would have been hanging around Eli, and he was inadvertently feeling his sister's depression. The depression probably was never his. How do you explain that to someone?

This is one of the many reasons it's so critical to cross over the dead.

Veronica, Eli's wife, suddenly interjected, "One day after work, Eli came home and swooped in and scooped me up and shouted, 'I love you!' and told me he felt so happy and light, and he had no idea why. We talked about this last night and all day today. This is a true miracle. When you crossed Emily over, you somehow saved a part of Eli's soul because some part of him knew that his sister had left him for a better place.

"Eli's depression was that he knew his sister was with him. He would question if she was haunting him to punish him for their last argument. It tortured him for all of these years. But now, I have my husband back. For the first time ever," she started to cry.

"Eli, you must realize that Emily was never mad at you," I said. "She never mentioned you two had an argument. The truth was she was stuck between dimensions. I'm so happy for you and your family. I'm also amazed at how this has unfolded and how you knew something had shifted for the better."

I was grateful for Eli's validation. Often, I don't receive confirmation that the services I perform are felt or noticed. Through this experience, I grew as much as Eli did.

"When you come back for the high school reunion, you *have* to come and visit us," they told me.

I was so happy for Eli. I can't imagine the torture that must have been for him, knowing that his last words to his sister were argumentative.

Three months later, I flew to Michigan to attend my high school reunion, and I visited Eli and Veronica at their home. It was an adorable home full of love. As we sat in their kitchen and talked, I suddenly noticed a ghost standing in the corner looking at me.

## Meet Mr. Brown

"Did you know you have a ghost in your home," I asked them. "And he is standing over there watching us?"

"Oh yes, he came with the house," said Veronica. "His name is Mr. Brown. He likes to watch over us and takes care of things."

"That's interesting. I have a question for you both," I said. "Do you happen to have plumbing issues or problems with appliances breaking down or other maintenance issues?"

There was stone-cold silence, and I knew by their expressions that I was on point. I may have heard their jaws hit the floor.

"Yes, why do you ask," Eli said. "I just had to replace the water heater, which was only five years old."

"The energy or frequency of a ghost is low, and because of that, mechanical or electrical operations issues can suddenly manifest," I said. "The low frequency of a ghost can inadvertently cause well-functioning items to break down quicker. I recommend that you cross him over. Here is a Crossing Over Prayer card that you can use. Just say the prayer, say it like you mean it, and instruct him to cross over. Honestly, it's the most compassionate act to do. It's no different than my sending Emily Home."

"Wow," said Eli. "We never thought of that. I have to be honest: I think I would miss Mr. Brown. He's kind of a part of the house. I need to think about this."

"Ok, if you need help crossing him over, just call. I don't have to be in the same room. We can do it over the phone," I told them as I left.

I got in my rental car, which I loved. When I exited the plane, I rented the most inexpensive car I could find. I mean, it was just me, and we had three little mouths to feed at home on one income now, and saving money was important.

But when I got inside the world's cheapest car rental, it reeked of cigarette smoke. I had demanded an odor-free car. The only one they had was a convertible Camaro. This car was awesome. It's completely different from my minivan life in San Diego. Even in the rain, I had the top down just for fun.

I was still in their driveway, about to pull onto the road, when I noticed him. He was sitting in the passenger's seat with the straightest pose. He was neatly dressed in a tucked-in flannel shirt and some work jeans.

It was Mr. Brown. I was stunned.

"Miss, do you mind," he said. "You can call me Mr. Brown," he said. "I heard you talking to the family in the house about going to Heaven, and I would like to go. When I first died, I didn't want to leave my home. I loved it so much and loved my family, children, and grandchildren. I have been able to watch them all grow up, but now, nothing is left for me here. Could you help me, please? I would be most grateful."

"Of course," I told him. He was so proper it was kind of funny.

"But wait," said Mr. Brown. "If you don't mind, miss. Could you please do me the honor of driving me around town for a bit?"

Ok, I have seen some weird situations in my life, but this one took the cake. I was now a chauffeur for a ghost. Driving Miss Daisy has nothing to do with this situation.

As I was driving around my hometown, this super lovely and proper ghost man sat beside me in my rented convertible, asking me for one last tour of the town before I crossed him over. My first thought was, I hope he doesn't blow out of the convertible because I am NOT putting the top up on this black beauty. Could he possibly blow out of my car? How does this work? He's a ghost, and there is no physical weight to hold him here.

I decided I would find out.

"Please turn right here," he said. "What a wonderful airport. It was built to help the farmers with crops and for crop dusting."

This airport was near the high school that I attended, the same high school where my dad was a history teacher. Mr. Brown instructed me to turn the car around in the parking lot.

"Could you please turn left here," he said. "And now, down this street to the right. This is unbelievable. These downtown buildings are still in great shape. This is astounding!"

I continued to drive him around for a bit more, and then I had to tell him I needed to cross him over because I would be late getting to see my stepmom and her friends.

"Oh, dear. I am so sorry to have kept you," said Mr. Brown." I want to thank you for your patience, kindness, and time. And I suppose it is time for you to do whatever you do to help me go to Heaven. I have been a faithful Christian and had such a wonderful life. I have been given more than I deserve, but I have also appreciated it. Thank you again, miss."

And with that, I had pulled off the road and into the parking lot of the VFW in Dowagiac and crossed him over. I marveled at how polite and kind he was. I had no idea why he wanted a tour of the town I grew up in, but I felt obliged to show him around for some reason.

Later that same evening, I attended my high school reunion and had a great time with friends I had not seen in a long time. I ran into Eli and told him Mr. Brown hopped into my car. He said he and his wife saw him leave with me and were happy for him.

I never told them about the private tour I gave their ghostly resident before I crossed him over. I was concerned they would think I was at least one fruit loop shy of a full bowl, if you know what I mean.

I returned home to San Diego, satisfied that I had tied up loose ends with Emily's family. The unexpected bonus was not only helping my dear friend's twin brother by crossing over his sister but also removing Mr. Brown's spiritual influence.

I happily resumed my not-so-normal family life.

After less than a week of being home, I got a surprise phone call from one of my best buds from school, Todd. We talked at the reunion all night long and had a great time. Todd is the kind of friend everyone needs in their life. His personality can convince you to try anything at least once. He's just a ton of fun and fabulous, positive energy.

## Another Twist

"Hey Laura, I got your number from Eli," said Todd. "I ran into him at the hardware store, and he told me an interesting story. By the way, I have my mom on the phone, too. And she says hi."

"Hi Martha, it's been years," I said. "A story? About Emily?"

"Yes, I did hear about Emily," said Todd. "Which is a cool story. But I want to talk to you about my grandfather."

"Who's that?" I asked.

"You mean you didn't know?" he asked.

"Know what? I'm really confused," I said.

"My grandfather built Eli and Veronica's house and the entire subdivision," he said. "The house they currently live in is the same house my grandfather lived in. My grandfather left in your car."

"What? Your grandfather was Mr. Brown. Are you kidding me?" I was astonished.

"Yep! That's him," he said.

"Wait a minute," I said. "You just told me he built that house and the subdivision. This is making sense now. I had no idea this was your grandfather, and I didn't know he was a builder. Boy, do I have a story for you? When I left Eli and Veronica's home, he had me drive him to the airport. Did he build that, too?"

"Yes, he did," he said.

"Then he had me take him all over downtown and to a few other nearby places," I said. "Was your grandfather also the developer for those areas, too?"

"Yes, he did." Both answered simultaneously.

"But Laura. I need to tell you something. Something huge," said Martha. "I know the exact *moment* you crossed over my father. I could *feel* it. He died about 20 years ago, and I have always known in my heart of hearts that he never went to Heaven, and that was devastating for me.

"I don't know why he didn't cross over into the Kingdom of God. Why didn't that happen? What did he do wrong? I have been so worried about his soul for so long. He was such a good and kind man. I don't understand it."

"Martha, first of all, your dad is probably one of the kindest men I have ever met, living or dead," I said. "He didn't cross over because he did something bad or wrong or God somehow judged him. He didn't cross over because he didn't want to die. He felt like he had so much more life to live, and he was grieving the loss of the life he lived.

"He loved his life and the people in it. It was as if he loved every moment of it. He didn't want it to end. He didn't know what to do when the light came for him. He just wanted to stay a bit longer. But then, when the light disappeared, he became stuck between dimensions," I explained.

"Laura, you have no idea how you changed my life," said Martha. "I have been so worried about him for so long. No one at our church knew how to help him. It has been heart-breaking. Why don't people know how to help the dead? Why is it that when someone like my dad doesn't cross over, people think he did something wrong and doesn't deserve to go to Heaven?" she screamed.

I suppose all those years of anger, frustration, grief, and sadness had been bottled up in her for years. She said she had a constant and chronic sense of sadness and depression. When her father crossed over, she felt her life looked brighter. She called it a miracle. And I suppose, in a sense, it was a miracle.

At this juncture, I started to fully appreciate the concept of soul health and soul transition.

These physical bodies we are all given are temporary housing units for the soul. Mr. Brown's love of his construction company started me on a quest to learn more about paranormal influences in our lives.

The twists and turns this true story took were amazing to me in so many ways. I will always cherish the childhood memories of Emily and the tour I gave Mr. Brown.

Or was it the tour that Mr. Brown gave me?

# Section II

...•◆•...

# MAKING SENSE
# OF IT ALL

# LET'S MAKE THE WORLD
# A BETTER PLACE

Every person and every profession or government entity that employs people has a personal responsibility to act in a manner that improves the human condition on Earth. Most have an idea of how to do that task.

Just observe our politics during an election, and you will find opinions abound on what should be done or said. Some of us have a heightened sense of worldly ownership and take leadership roles. Some people are comfortable telling others what to think or how to live. I have decided to educate many people on a spiritual path with God as my Source to improve our time here.

Many years ago, I decided to follow in my father's footsteps to become a public school teacher. My path is not as linear as his was, but I would like to think that he showed me how to be a selfless educator and supporter of humanity. In this book, through my talks, and in my private counseling sessions, I continue teaching my students and clients how karma works with spiritual attainment and personal practices.

My learning came from others as they learned from others. I had great teachers, some of whom are mentioned in this book. Rarely are there any original ideas, just a fresh approach to present what we instinctively know to be true.

I don't teach "religion," for that concept can be found in churches, synagogues, temples, and mosques. I teach how to be better participants at those churches, synagogues, temples, and mosques. I have learned the processes. I have acquired the tools. I have consciously decided to dedicate the rest of my life to sharing with you what our creator has shared with me – and that is to enhance our spiritual performance while inhabiting this physical planet for the greater societal good of every breathing soul who collectively resides on Earth.

What does it mean "to make the world a better place?" Recycling? Cleaning up the land and oceans? Animal conservation? Personal responsibility? Have our corporations, politicians, and governments do a better job at their jobs?

The answer is yes to all these, but it's much more. By looking at all aspects of our lives from our families, professions, play, work, and leisure time – we can't escape the fact that we are spiritual beings inhabiting a physical body. However, consequences come with spiritual experiences. We have discovered that not all spiritual experiences are good or come from the true God Source. That is when we learn the most about our true selves, our intentions, and the courage it takes to stay genuine for the greater good.

Spirituality can also be compared to a harmonic scale. In its most basic form, a harmonic scale is a "super-just" musical scale. A harmonic is a frequency, and a frequency is a vibration. Frequencies fluctuate on the harmonic scale, as in music.

When you study music, you study harmonic scales. Every note and tone vibrates at a different frequency. Sometimes, these notes work well together, and we get a beautiful chord, and sometimes, they sound so awful it hurts our ears. The key to spirituality is understanding what it means to raise vibration and create harmonies.

For example, think about your favorite song. Every time you listen to it, you feel good. It brings back memories of time, places, and loved ones. Some songs create anxiety and espouse violence, where they have messages of rape and destruction. Where do these songs fit on the harmonic scale of spirituality?

I love many songs, but there is one in particular that I really, genuinely love, and here's why. One night, when my baby was about one year old, she couldn't sleep, which was not all that unusual. Naturally, being a new mom, I picked her up to comfort her. As I did that, all I could think of was how exhausted I would be the following day and that I had to teach middle school. I was a bit annoyed at the time. I just wanted to sleep.

It was just after midnight, and I was holding my baby girl tightly in my arms when I walked outside and turned on the radio. I immediately noticed the moon was unusually large, and the moonlight was bright. Everything looked clear. Looking at my daughter, I could see her entire face clearly, and she was incredibly happy. It was as if we had a few stolen moments together. Immediately, my tired frustrations melted away, and I was in the moment with my daughter.

Unexpectedly, she grabbed both sides of my face, and with her tiny hands, she kissed me. The song playing at that exact moment on the radio was _Kiss Me_ by Sixpence None the Richer. Instantly, I fell in love again with this beautiful tiny human, my first-born daughter.

Music has a magical ability to anchor us in time. Every time I hear that song, I'm immediately transported back to that moment in time, and I marvel at what a wonderful person she has become and how quickly time passes. At that moment, my baby taught me the importance of being in the moment and what unconditional love feels like on a whole new level. Perhaps you also have a favorite song that brings back memories of a favorite moment or a favorite person.

We must understand that creativity is the spark of life, a gift from God. Creativity comes through us in many ways and forms. Music is only one form of creativity that God has gifted us.

What would it be like if there was no creativity or we lacked the free will to be creative, hone our skills, or not be able to grow our passions? What would that world look like?

Fundamentally, everything is spiritual—every object, thought, and action. Why? Because everything we experience comes from God.

We need to clean up this world in which we live. We are in a spiritual war, and we have been for many millennia. Learning to recognize the spiritual forces that do us harm and how to protect ourselves will go a long way in enhancing our spiritual path. Luciferic forces have wreaked havoc on us, and it's time we learn to take our power back.

Each of us has the power to make the world a better place. It can be as simple as picking up a piece of trash, having compassion for an animal who needs help, or caring for an ill loved one. We have to study the dark to learn about the light. Doctors study all sorts of diseases, bacteria, and viruses to use their knowledge to bring their patients back to good health. To the light. God is light, and there is no healing without God.

Every culture throughout the history of this planet has words, terms, and concepts for ghosts, demons, and angels. Ghosts, demons, and other dark entities exist in the fourth dimension. We need to understand this logic trail.

The beings that reside in the fourth dimension have proven to impact our third-dimensional reality. It's as if there is a subtle- and sometimes not too subtle- overlay between the $3^{rd}$ and $4^{th}$ dimensions. If you recall, the third dimension is the dimension in which we live. It's our physical world. All those elements that consist of our beautiful planet.

The beings that reside in the $4^{th}$ dimension know that they can and do have a direct impact on our lives. This impact is not for our greater good. When Lucifer and his team fell from the Heavens, they had to go *somewhere*. They also needed a new energy source. They no longer had access to the light/energy of the higher dimensions. We mortals were not prepared for what was to come. I question if the light side knew what was about to happen.

In all my time crossing over souls who found themselves stuck between Heaven and Earth, I have had the honor and privilege of learning a lot from them. Many times, the dead are held captive by dark entities and not allowed to cross over to go Home.

Think about that for a moment. We should never, ever assume that a loved one who passes went Home and is in a better place. Instead, we should actively ensure that a loved one (or even a not-so-loved one) crosses over and is in the hands of the Divine, God, Source, or whatever you want to call it.

# IN THE NAME OF GOD, JESUS, ALLAH, AND BUDDHA

D uring these challenging times, our home became the epicenter of a spiritual war. The prize: to take me out. This was never anything I could have ever predicted or imagined.

When we think of war, we have certain physical constructs in mind. We can see the battle with our eyes. We can hear it with our ears. You get the idea. What happens when the war you are fighting is in another *dimension?* How do you handle that? How do you protect yourself and your loved ones when you can't see the enemy? You can't see the forces you are trying to fight against or, at the very least, safeguard yourself against. It's not a level playing field. It's not fair. And it doesn't matter.

It's a karmic intrusion, and it's an opportunity. It is an opportunity to learn, to figure some things out, to figure out the elements of the unimaginable.

It's important to understand that churches, synagogues, and other religious institutions have their place in humanity. I believe in their positive effects. All the holy texts have many common elements, and it's essential to understand this. The following are my experiences with searching for help.

Although they are my experiences, they also offered many powerful lessons.

Every day, I sought help on this battleground that greatly impacted my family, home, and life. Every day, I would talk to someone new and try something new, and nothing worked. I was told so many things that made no sense, like burning a black candle, which would absorb all the dark entities in your home. What kind of power does a colored wax and a small flame have? In fact, at times, those things I would try sometimes made matters worse.

"Command that the dark beings leave your home and say it with authority." I was told. While I wanted them to leave, I didn't want them to become someone else's problem. But we desperately needed a reprieve from the constant and chronic torture we were enduring.

"In the name of God, in the name of Jesus, in the name of Allah, in the name of Buddha, I command all dark entities to leave this property RIGHT NOW!" I screamed over and over. However, when I ordered them and demanded them to leave and leave us alone, it only escalated the paranormal activity in our house.

It was straight out of a horror movie: cabinet doors flung open, artwork fell off the walls, and our poor animals ran outside through the doggie door.

I would constantly ask myself, "Why is this so hard? Why is there no information on this stuff?" When it came to my "spiritual war" checklist, the only items I routinely ever seemed to cross off were what didn't work.

I was constantly looking for help from psychics and spiritual practitioners, religious clergy, and anything that would help me move this needle. I was coming at this from all the angles I could possibly imagine.

"Where do you go to church? Now that our girls are getting older, we are looking for a new church." Or "Since we just moved here, we are looking for a closer church." I would ask these types of questions to anyone I could. I wasn't trying to be intentionally deceitful. Still, we so badly needed relief, and who knows, maybe finding a friendly church family would have been a welcome change from our current existence.

I would find the names and phone numbers of religious institutions and call them. I made the calls during the days while the kids were at school. I could no longer simultaneously hold down a job and fight this unprecedented war, so I left my teaching career.

Here is what I did know about religious institutions: They are man-made constructs that are hopefully altruistic in their ability to connect people to God, GodSource, or whatever label you want to put on it. I also know there are people in religious institutions who use their power as a form of control over others.

Navigating religious waters could be as perilous as navigating psychic waters. The only weapon I came armed with was my intuition. Learning to trust my intuition and learn to listen to myself, I knew, would be the key to saving my family's soul.

"You were referred to me as someone who could help me with an unusual problem," I stated. This was the beginning line of pretty much every phone call I would make over two years. This sentence was etched into my exhausted, sleep-deprived brain. The ability to have a lengthy and coherent conversation was getting harder and harder.

Somewhere along the way, sleep switched from a necessity to a luxury.

## A Child of the Devil

"What would you like help with?" he asked me.

This was a pastor at a local protestant parish. I had heard through the grapevine that this man was compassionate and wise. My neighbor gave me his number as they had been attending this church for years. I was hopeful he had some insights or could point me in some helpful direction.

"We have a lot of ghosts and other entities in our house, and they keep harassing one of my kids. I'm desperate, and I don't know what to do." I said as I worked hard to hold back my tears. Each day was getting harder and harder to deal with. Nothing ever let up. EVER.

His response was not what I expected. I expected this man 'of the cloth' to have some compassion, wisdom, or guidance. Instead, the calm and sweet "Hello" he initially greeted me instantly became an accusatory rage.

"If your daughter can see these things, that means she is the child of the devil. The devil works through the weak and the misguided. She is the one who is bringing this to your family. She is the one who is destroying your family. She is symbolically the root of all evil." He continued screaming at me. Good grief, this was a challenging and devastating phone call.

It was as if, somehow, his words got blocked out of my mind after the first few sentences. I could not process what he was saying, and I was so shocked that I was frozen and couldn't hang up my phone for the longest time. I don't remember putting down the phone. It was as if I blanked out, and his words put me into some type of catatonic state.

The next thing I remembered was being curled up into a ball on my sofa and crying. I don't know how I got there. I didn't know what to expect with calling this pastor. But I did know I never expected this man, this supposed representative of God, to crush what little hope and spirit I had left.

How could this man, this supposed man of God, tell me that my sweet and kind little girl was a child of the devil, the devil's spawn? What right did he have to tell me those things? If he couldn't help me, why couldn't he say that?

This man's level of cruelty was beyond my comprehension and belief system, all in the "name of God." Until I wrote about this, I had never told anyone what he had told me. My family didn't need to know about this. Our daughters didn't need to know this. Enough was happening, which would have only caused our family more harm. (As I write this, I cry all over again with this memory. But thankfully, it's just a memory now.)

## Making This Up for Attention

The Unitarians are, in general, a friendly bunch of people. Inclusive, loving, bring a potluck dish to pass, and you are in. We have several friends who go to a couple of different Unitarian churches, and, in the past, we had attended a few different types of services, like Christenings and weddings. If religions had rainbows, this would be where they were made. My encounters had all been so positive and inclusive.

This time, I decided to find a Unitarian church outside my county. My rationale was to create an added layer of protection because it would be harder to find me if this person were far away. It sounds so illogical now, but at the time, it made sense. It probably made sense because the sleep deprivation was taking a more profound toll on me.

"Maybe, just maybe, this institution won't be so judgmental." I had told my confidant, half laughing and half fearful of what may come out of this.

"We have nothing to lose." Was his only response.

We both secretly just wanted to shove this issue under the rug, but that wasn't possible. Those scary and ugly monsters always found their way out and came back to haunt us with even more vengeance.

The next day, I called this Unitarian church in another county.

"She's six years old, about to enter first grade, and incredibly psychic. We are finding that all of these different types of entities are coming at her day and night. A lot of them are ghosts, but many of them are a lot worse than ghosts. I don't understand what they are or how to make them disappear." I told Lana, the Unitarian Minister and the only female religious person I contacted.

I decided to tell her about two specific and ongoing events. The first one was the glaring ghost issue. The second one was rather strange: the three-headed crocodile.

Yes, you read that right. This three-headed crocodile would roam around our house day and night. It was about 2-3 feet long. This 'thing,' as I had no other words for it, had been residing with us for a few months.

As I continued to share this with Lana, I had a hard time believing it myself. Hearing me say these works out loud, I felt like a nut job, but I also knew it was the truth. This was one of those many low points I had to deal with.

Lana never said a word. I wondered if she was thinking I was the nut job that I sounded like or if she believed me. Or that I was some radio jockey pulling a prank on her. I reiterated the following story that happened a few months prior:

"Mo-oooom!!!" My daughter was screaming over and over and standing on her bed, pointing at the floor.

"Don't come in! There is a giant three-headed crocodile in here! He's right there! And he has yellow and red eyes!" She was shrieking and shaking as I ran into her room.

My daughter was pointing to the side of her bed where this non-physical creature appeared to her. I ran to the foot of her bed, scooped up my little girl, and slammed the door shut. But I quickly realized this non-physical entity could walk through doors and walls. It followed us to the dining room as my daughter was reporting to me that its long, scaly tail was swishing back and forth, its beady red and yellow eyes were staring at us, and it would open its mouth just enough so she could see its razor-sharp teeth and then it disappeared. . . for a while.

Lana seemed quite interested in our story, so I continued. While I never saw this entity with my own two physical eyes, I knew when it was around. It terrified not only my daughter but our pets, too. This is how I knew what she was seeing was real. Our beloved pets somehow became the proverbial canaries in the coal mine.

Benny, our sweet little house-trained rabbit, would get backed into the corner as this beast terrorized him. The terror in our rabbit's eyes was heartbreaking. Rabbits normally do not vocalize. It's a survival instinct. Instead of making vocal sounds, when Benny would get backed into the corner by this scary entity, he would thump his foot on our hardwood floors, which carried throughout the house. When this happened, one of us would pick him up and hold him until things calmed down. Seeing how this sweet little rabbit was so tortured and there was not much I could do about it was heartbreaking.

Lana asked me, "How do you know the rabbit was thumping his foot out of fear?"

"This foot thumping was never an issue before," I said. "I know this sounds crazy, but we need help."

Because my animals were suffering, it made this more real. I viewed our pets as a placebo. They didn't know what we thought we knew. They lived it. When people talk about 'spirits,' they only seem to talk about angels and the good stuff. No one ever talks about this other stuff. Why? Probably because it makes us feel safe. But when you encounter this level of darkness, it can be really dangerous.

"What do you make of this? Have you ever heard of anything like this before? Do you know of anyone who can help us?" I asked her

Lana listened patiently, then said, "It sounds like your daughter is looking for attention. Do you and your husband want to come in for counseling?"

"We are looking for spiritual help with our situation," I said. Can you help us with this? We need more than just counseling."

"You need to see what your daughter lacks and why she needs to tell you such tales," Lana said in a very condescending tone.

When she said that, it was as if she stabbed me in my heart with a knife. The feeling of defeat was becoming more and more normal for me. I just hung up the phone and never responded to her offer of family counseling.

## What About an Exorcism?

From my understanding of the Catholic religion, they deal with ghosts and demons. Maybe, just maybe, they could be helpful. I had no expectations at this point.

I cold-called this Catholic church, and the Father answered immediately. I told him we weren't Catholic, but we were dealing with some unusual paranormal problems, and is this something they may be able to help us with? He put me in contact with a "special division" of the Catholic church. I can't remember what it was called, but a couple of days later, I got a phone call from someone in this institution who deals with the paranormal.

"Hello, is this Laura?" he asked me.

"Yes. May I ask who is calling?" I responded.

"This is Joe, and I am from the Mis-Information Division of the Catholic Church." Ok, his name is really not Joe, and there probably is no division of misinformation in the Catholic church. But that's how it felt. Plus, names have been changed out of respect and privacy, and I honestly can't remember where he said he was from.

Joe began to educate me, "The term ghost comes from the word poltergeist, which means noisy spirit. These ghosts and other non-saints may annoy people but can never harm them. I must come to your house and bless your home with Holy Water. Then, if this doesn't work, I will need to do an exorcism on your daughter," he said.

"Wait. What? An exorcism on my minor daughter?" I asked. A sense of rage overcame me. She is terrified enough, but to do God knows what to her? I imagined this stranger strapping her into some type of chair, and I said to myself, "Over my dead body!"

I calmed myself down quickly because rage is never anyone's friend. Rage will overshadow wisdom and insight. I took a deep breath to steady myself, not wanting to offend this man who was trying to be helpful.

"If they can never harm us, then why does my daughter get knife marks on her little body from a ghost," I asked. "I thought exorcisms were about entities that take over a person's soul. There aren't entities *inside* of her. They are all over our house. Why would you want to add more trauma to her and our family like that? I am searching for help and knowledge on how to deal with this issue."

"I mean this with all sincerity. How does Holy Water work?" I asked. "Once it evaporates, do these entities come back? Where do they go when the holy water is put on them? Do you spray it all over the house? Does it work in conjunction with a blessing?" My mind raced with more questions.

"Ma'am, your daughter is the problem," he said. "She is attracting demons because she is not rooted in the Body of Christ."

"My daughter is the problem," I asked. "Did you *really* just say that?" It was all I could do to not jump through the phone line and throttle this guy. "I am sorry, but none of what you are saying makes sense. Let's start with what Holy Water is and how it works. What happens to those entities that get touched by it?"

"Holy water has been blessed by a priest using consecrated salt." He said in a very matter-of-fact tone.

"So, if I continually spritz my daughter with holy water, we should be good to go," I asked. I was being serious.

It was as if his mission was to convince me this was the correct protocol. My problem was he could never answer my question about what happens to these entities, where they go, or whether they will return. These questions I had about where "do they go" is the crux of the matter.

If they get banished, do they go to my neighbor's house? Do they now become someone else's problem? I don't want to be responsible for someone else's torture if these beings latch on to another person or family. What about the myriad of child ghosts that are now residing with us? What about Herman or the devilish Annabelle? To me, these souls still needed to be helped. I didn't know how or what that meant.

This was going nowhere fast. He obviously didn't know the answers to my questions. He acted like a telemarketer who was given a script. Feeling the advice of this well-meaning Catholic priest would not work, I gratefully ended the phone call, knowing our problem was no closer to being solved.

## Anoint Your Windows and Doors with This Special Oil

In our research on religions, I came across the Mormon religion as one that believes in ghosts and other entities. Our community has so many Mormon churches that there is even one for the Spanish-speaking population. Fortunately, I had a friend whose husband was one of the higher-ups of this institution.

I casually asked her out for breakfast under the guise of catching up. During our meeting, I asked her about Mormon beliefs regarding ghosts and other things, telling her I was just curious.

"Ghosts are disembodied evil spirits," she said. "It's said that Satan has converted one-third of the pre-mortals to evil. They now belong to him and not God. Any medium, psychic, or spiritualist who contacts them is a follower of Satan. They may not know it."

"So, anyone who can see or hear a ghost is connected to Satan?" I asked her. "If someone has a ghost in their house, does that mean they are connected to Satan? Is it possible to get rid of a ghost in a home then?"

"It's possible," she said. "A ghost can only enter a home when a person is in a spiritual crisis, though."

Spiritual crisis, well, that's an understatement, I thought. Do I say anything or not? If the Mormons have something that could help us with our situation, that would be great.

"How do you remove a ghost?" I asked her. I was debating whether to say anything about our ghost issue. Then, my intuition kicked in and screamed, "NO! Keep your mouth shut!" As I listened to my intuition, my friend kept talking.

"Most LDS men have this ability," she said. "All they need is a special oil to anoint a home and say a blessing." She was getting excited about this subject.

"Just the LDS men and not the women," I asked her. "How can that be? Does that make sense?" I hate to sound

blasphemous, but why on earth would only the male population have this ability? She had no response to my questions.

When our time ended, I thanked her for meeting me, and
she invited me to attend their church. While the offer was
nice, I knew there was a better fit for my family. Could you
imagine if this entire community found out we had ghosts in
our home and, therefore, we must be labeled Satanists?

## We Have to Keep Trying

Someone who knew someone who knew a little bit about our
predicament told me about yet another Catholic church that
could help us. She gave me a phone number to the home of
a Catholic priest, Father Jacob. She told me I should call him
because he has a team of spiritual leaders that cross over the
dead into Heaven and could help us with Annabelle.

I was elated! I remembered thinking that this might actually work. I called Father Jacob, who requested that my husband and I meet with him the next day.

Leaving my kids home alone or with a babysitter for any
moment was a terrifying thought.

I remember the last time that happened. We were at our
neighbors' for dinner. We had only been next door for maybe
30 minutes when I got a phone call from my daughter. They
were freaked out because a glass on the table flew off and
shattered. She said no one was in the dining room at the time.
When this happened, we were right next door.

How am I going to manage to leave them home for an
hour? I prayed and prayed hard that my daughters would
be safe while we were gone to meet this priest who could
help us.

I was not fully honest with Father Jacob. I decided only to tell him about Annabelle, one issue at a time. Annabelle seemed like the most straightforward issue to resolve with the most significant benefit. The other crazy stuff was just way too much. But if he could help us with Annabelle, then I could tell him a bit more.

My husband and I were invited into Father Jacob's home. It was small and quaint. He kindly offered us some tea, had us sit at his small, round table, and asked us to tell him what was happening.

"We have had a ghost child living with us for almost two years now," I said. "She started out nice, and somewhere along the way, she has become vicious and cruel. This ghost is focusing all of her energy on one of our daughters. We don't know what to do with her or about this situation. We have tried so many things, and nothing works."

"We have a spiritual ministry team that is made up of three women who assist me with these unusual problems," he said. "But first, I need you to answer some questions to help you better."

We spent the next hour reviewing my husband's and my family's backgrounds. He was interested in any religions we or our family members may have belonged to. Then, an interesting question came up—a question that took my husband and me both by surprise.

He looked at me and asked, "Have you ever had an abortion?"

I was quite taken aback but told him, "No. I have never had an abortion. Why?"

He ignored my question of why and proceeded to ask both my husband and me if we knew of any family member who had an abortion. That's when my husband mentioned that one of his sisters (who is now deceased) had an abortion when she was a teenager. But that was 30 or 40 years ago.

"What does this have to do with Annabelle," I asked him.

"It's quite possible that Annabelle is the disincarnated spirit of that aborted baby," he said.

"How can that be possible," I asked. "Annabelle is presenting herself to us as a seven-year-old girl. I don't understand how this works."

"Any child who has been aborted roams the spirit land," he said. "Annabelle is one of those disincarnated spirits. I will call my ministry team, and we will set a date to do a high mass. Thank you for coming." He said as we left.

"Ok, that was weird." I had told my husband in the car.

"Leave it to the Catholics to turn something like this into an abortion issue." My husband said, laughing once the car doors were shut and we were out of earshot.

"I can't believe that this guy somehow decided that our paranormal issues are because your sister had an abortion more than 40 years ago," I said. "Why would this aborted fetus come back to haunt us as a seven-year-old child ghost? Why wouldn't the then fetus be haunting your sister or the father? Plus, when we told him that this ghost child died in a car accident, he brushed that off. What should we do? Should we cancel this high mass? This doesn't sound right."

"We need to try at least," said my husband. "If they can get Annabelle out of our lives and into Heaven, we can put aside the crazy abortion notion."

"Ok, let's see what happens," I told him when we were in the driveway.

Four days later, I got a call from Father Jacob. "I spoke with his ministry team, and we will meet Tuesday night for a High Mass for Annabelle at 6:30 p.m. We would like for you and your entire family to come."

"Alright, I will let my husband know. Thank you very much," I said.

Tuesday arrived, and I told my daughters we had plans this evening.

"You mean they are going to get rid of Annabelle for me," said my daughter. "She won't bug me anymore?" my little girl squealed delightfully. I can't remember the last time she was happy. The idea that Annabelle could no longer be able to harass or harm my little girl was the best news we had in so long.

"What do you mean you are running late?" I asked my husband.

"We have a last-minute meeting with the higher-ups on this new release, and I can't get out of the meeting," he told me.

"We're all supposed to be here. You are the one who wanted to follow through with this. And now you aren't coming?" I was angry.

I rounded up our daughters and Annabelle. She liked to go on car rides with us, hoping she would somehow find her parents. It was sad and depressing. But this time, Annabelle knew she might be able to go to Heaven, and she was excited about that.

Sometimes, I can't believe the conversations we have in our house.

When we entered the church, we were greeted by Father Jacob, who introduced us to the three women who were his spiritual ministers. There were six chairs in a semi-circle set up at the altar. As we walked in, Father Jacob instructed us that the girls would sit in the pews and I would sit in one of the chairs at the altar between Father Jacob and the three women. As they removed the chair for my husband, I tried not to roll my eyes. I was not happy he wasn't there, but I knew it couldn't be avoided.

As we took our places, Father Jacob told us what would happen: They would do a high mass for Annabelle, and then the women would cross her over. I remember being excited about this prospect. As much as Annabelle was a destructive little force, I wanted to get her the help she needed for her sake and ours.

When the high mass finished, we were asked to close our eyes in prayer for Annabelle. That's when things got interesting. These three women became incredibly animated. I peeked at them with one eye to see what was going on. They were sitting in their chairs, rocking and rolling back and forth. I was kind of concerned that one of them might fall off their chair.

"I see Annabelle. She's in the meadow and frolicking in the grass," said one of the spiritual ministers seated beside me. I was slightly concerned her flailing arms would hit me.

"Oh, I see her, too. She is there," said another spiritual minister.

"She is so happy here." Relayed the third spiritual minister.

"I can now see Jesus!" said the spiritual minister next to me. "Annabelle is running to him. And she is now in his arms. They are having a joyous reunion."

These three women tried to convince me that what was happening was real, as if they had rehearsed this script. The conversation continued for at least 15 minutes about what a wonderful reunion this was.

At one point, I looked at my daughters. Two of them were staring wide-eyed in bewilderment. I could see that my third daughter, Annabelle, found this all highly entertaining. My daughter had her hand cupped over her mouth and was shaking so hard, with tears streaming down her face while she was looking at the 'empty' seat next to her. I gave her that 'mom look' that told her to knock it off.

When they finished, they told us how grateful they were to have helped Annabelle and, of course, come to services this Sunday. I thanked them for their help, for which I was sincere. They all took time out of their day to help us in the best way they knew possible.

At the same time, I could not get my girls in the car fast enough. Once we were in the car, we all laughed and laughed for the longest time. Why? Because Annabelle was still in the car with us.

Every situation offers us a learning opportunity. In my quest for help, I encountered many different philosophies from many well-intentioned professionals. My experiences with these religions could have been better, even though most were genuinely trying to help. We sought the holiest of cures, yet in each case, the solutions we sought escaped us.

What this says about organized man-centered religion could be one of the many reasons why church attendance is decreasing in American society today. Where are the real solutions? I asked myself this question after every failed session with these people.

What I didn't grasp at the time was that these failures were the best learning experiences I could have faced. I learned what was real and what was not. I should qualify that last statement: nothing in the spiritual realm seems natural when going through it. The reality is we have to learn. We must understand that the paranormal is much more normal than we think. It influences all of us daily. Only most of us don't know what is happening.

# THE PSYCHIC CIRCUS

I t was one of those emotional moments that melded anger, frustration, and fear into one giant ball in the pit of my stomach. The "hat-man" returned. His reappearance sickened every fiber of my body, including my inner psyche and mental being. He might have been gone for a month, maybe a couple of weeks, or perhaps only a week. I don't remember. I just remembered we gained a reprieve with the "hat-man's" absence.

That's the issue with chronic fatigue: You start to lose your mind, or at least think you are losing your mind. Now I know why sleep deprivation is used as a form of torture. All I knew then was that this "hat-man" was not a ghost. For some reason, ghosts were not as unnerving as this being.

The "hat-man" was a type of being with no known entity origin that I could decipher despite my exhausting attempts to learn about the unseen spiritual world as much as possible. He just wore a fedora-style hat. What I *did* know was he was not here for our collective greater good. He would appear in the corner of my daughter's room and not move. He just stared as if he was taking in information. I demanded that my daughter never, ever engage with him. My intuition screamed with repulsion, yet I was powerless to remove him.

Finding help for our problem wasn't easy. I drained all the local churches and spent thousands of dollars on psychics and spiritual practitioners. Telling people about the "gifts" my little girl possessed was not always a welcomed conversation starter. Once, I remember my good friend whose kid made the all-stars for soccer. She was excited as she shared the news, while I remained mute about our daughter's "talents" to protect her from other's scorn. I had to psych myself up to attend this PTA meeting where my overly abundant joyful friend would be bubbling at the excitement of her little All-Star. Her "gifted" kid.

The previous year, I agreed to oversee a few school events and was also elected to some PTA committees. To this day, I honestly don't remember which position I was elected to.

I was so tired. I did know this. I had to get ready for that meeting. My prep work for the meeting consisted of organizing plans and documents, hiding the dark circles under my eyes with what seemed like a half pound of concealer, and summoning a fake and happy smile on my face. Then, taking a deep breath, I entered the PTA meeting with my "New Normal Persona."

At this Back-to-School PTA event, my bubbly friend asked other moms if they knew of good personal coaches to help her daughter gain some soccer skills. I wanted to cry. Everyone was so excited for her, and I never felt so alone with our family secret. If any of these people knew what we were dealing with, we would have been considered pariah material. After all, they used to burn witches for more benign activities.

One other item I took to this PTA meeting was this sticky note I wrote to myself with a green colored pencil. It's funny what odd and inconsequential details we remember at times. I tried to muster seemingly idle chit-chat at the meeting with dozens of parents. I had this note folded in my pocket, and I held it like some security blanket.

My secret note read:

*"That's great your kid is a star athlete, straight A student, and good-looking.*

*My kid talks to dead people, is exhausted, and chronically late for school."*

I felt like a failure as a mom. Eventually, I tore up that note without uttering a single word.

When a normal child has an amazing ability, excelling at soccer or playing the piano, that parent can go around and ask other parents, "Hey, do you know of a good soccer coach?" or "Can you recommend a piano teacher?" Those parents can even brag about how great their kid is at their so-called "gift."

If you have an exceptionally psychic child and you need help, you can't go around asking, "Do you know of any good psychics? My child sees some weird stuff, and I want to help her. Do you know of anyone?" If you are a teacher in that same school, you don't want to ask about this.

In searching for help, I started by doing internet searches on ghosts, ghost removal, spirits, etcetera. You named it, and I searched for it. All the websites I encountered looked dark, unprofessional, and, frankly, dangerous. I couldn't pinpoint what was dangerous about them at the time. They just felt wrong.

I then started feeling out certain friends I attributed to being more 'open' with certain concepts and ideas. I was quietly asking people if they knew of a psychic or someone where I could get a reading and that type of service.

A considerable part of my problem was I lacked a lot of the necessary vocabulary in this area. Defining the help or words I sought and what my family desperately needed was as foreign as the entities occupying my home. I had a few friends who gave me some numbers, and I called them and spent a lot of money on these odd services, looking for that elusive help.

I would call these psychics and ask them questions about what they knew about psychic children. I would tell them a little, only that my daughter could see ghosts. "Do you have any ideas on how I can help her? These ghosts seem to like her, and it's draining."

That seemed to be the most benign aspect of these events. Ghosts were now ordinary for us. Almost all these psychics had my greater good in mind—almost all. I'll get to that *almost* part in a bit. The one common thread with these psychics is they wanted to give her a label and stick her up on some silly ego-boosting pedestal.

**Psychic #1:** "Oh, you are so fortunate, you have a Star Seed Child."

"Fortunate? How so," I asked.

"A star seed child is one who comes from the higher realms for a specific purpose to heal the earth." said Psychic #1.

"Um-ok," I said. "I'm just trying to help her attend enough school so she can pass the first grade."

**Psychic #2:** "I can see she is an Indigo Child."

"What does that mean," I asked.

"She possesses unusual abilities, and there is a school she can attend to help her grow her abilities."

"Um-ok, I said. "I'm just trying to help her be able to sleep at night and not be bothered by all of these ghosts."

**Psychic #3:** "She is a child of the Blue Ray, and she needs guidance, and I can help her." "Blue Ray, like the DVDs?" I asked, half-joking.

"No, these children that come to us are special." Psychic #3 replied in all seriousness. "They are incredibly intuitive and need a lot of guidance, and I can help her with this."

"How can you help her exactly," I asked.

"You can bring her to my place, and I will educate her. We can start with one two-hour session per week."

"And where do I, her parent, fit into this picture?" I asked

"I only work with the child," said Psychic #3. "You can bring her to my home and wait in the car while I teach her how to expand her gifts."

I'm thinking so many thoughts by this point. The first is I hate the word "gift." And what parent in their right mind would drop their kid off at a stranger's house and LEAVE THEM THERE? On what flipping planet is that ever a good idea?

Then I met **Psychic #4.**

"There's not just ghosts in your house," said Psychic #4. "There's also a lot of demon-like entities, too. I can clearly see that. You are going to need to protect her, especially in school. The best way to do this is to sit in a lotus position in a comfortable place and surround your daughter in a sphere of white light while she is at school."

"For 6 ½ hours a day? Every day?" I asked.

"Yes, this will keep her safe," they said.

I wondered how I would find time to pay the bills, buy groceries, go to work, or do any other regular activity. This is all great in theory, but it is not practical in any way.

**Psychic #62:** "She is a part of the Rainbow group of children who are coming in now to help change the earth."

Click. I just hung up the phone on this woman. I just can't deal with these nut jobs. At the same time, I have to keep trying. Somewhere, there has to be some answer.

**Psychic #80:** "Just let her follow Spirit, and she will be fine."

"What exactly is Spirit," I asked. "And why should I let my little girl blindly follow Spirit?"

I'm a responsible parent. I would never let my daughter go to the park by herself or go to run after the man in the ice cream truck by herself. Why should I let her follow something I can't see? HOW ON EARTH IS THAT A GOOD IDEA?

Ironically, this person was from Rainbow, CA. I wonder if she knew the Rainbow psychic person. Seriously, I am not making this up.

**Psychic #584:** "She is a Blue Ray Star Seed Child and is a highly advanced soul."

**Me:** Click.

Along the way, we met one psychic who was an animal telepath. Out of all my daughter's abilities, animal communication was her favorite, and she wanted to meet someone who could talk to animals just like she could. She sincerely wanted to know if someone else on this planet was just like her.

My limited knowledge at the time is comical now. I remember searching for terms like "talking to animals" or "hearing animal thoughts." In the process, I found a woman who claimed to talk to animals, and after several discussions with her, we made an appointment to drive five hours to meet her.

It was disastrous.

When we arrived, she greeted us and asked us to come inside. She had several animals: a dog, two cats, some guinea pigs, and rabbits. It was a charming location. However, once we were inside, this grown woman suddenly started talking to my daughter and me in a baby voice, telling us that her animals were telling her that my daughter really couldn't communicate with animals and was making this all up.

She finished by literally calling my daughter a liar. However, I knew that my daughter could communicate with animals. There were too many instances in our own home that were proof enough.

Looking back, this animal communicator saw my seven-year-old as competitive and was cruel to my daughter. She kept telling us that this was all in my daughter's imagination and that maybe she should see a psychiatrist. What was interesting was the animals this woman kept didn't like her. They would run from her as she would approach them.

Even I could see this situation was twisted.

I was always present with my daughter at these meetings, and she was unkind to her. What would have happened if I hadn't been in the same room with her?

## And Then There Was Nancy

In the swirl of activity to find help, I had forgotten my friend Ellen. She had previously given me a number of a psychic that she had been using for years. I called and set up an appointment with her.

The psychic's name was Nancy, and she lived in Washington, D.C. Nancy was a cut above the rest. She was an entirely different mold from the myriads of psychics with whom I had been dealing. Most of them had our greater good in mind, but at the same time, they lacked a basic logic stream.

Nancy's calm voice drew me in. She was serious and meant business. Although I was still suffering from massive sleep deprivation, speaking with her was energizing.

I told her more about my family secret than anyone outside our immediate family. She was honest and said what we were dealing with was out of her league. I respected her honesty, but it also validated the largeness of the problem.

I wrote down what she said as she recorded our session. Later, she mailed me the cassette tape. One of the more significant impressions she mentioned was that I would meet a "woman in uniform." She would be able to help me, and we would end up being business partners. However, I also needed to have a discerning eye with the woman in uniform. While she would be helpful, she could 'turn dark' quickly.

I didn't know what she meant by a discerning eye. But for the first time since this drama started, I began to feel hopeful. I also forgot to ask her what kind of uniform.

Again, it's funny what sticks in your mind at specific points. This was one of those anchor points in this whole journey. "What kind of uniform? A McDonald's uniform? Mailman? Police officer? Nurse? There are so many uniforms out there." And with that, I forgot about her comment for another 18 long months.

After spending all these months searching for help, one haunting reality remained—the "hat-man" still occupied our home. We still had no reprieve from "Annabelle the Terror" and the myriads of other entities that became our alternate reality. I was no closer to finding the help we all needed—or so I thought.

# THE SAGE EXPERIMENT

This four-letter "S" word often comes up when dealing with the paranormal. "S" is for Sage, and it seems to be coveted as the holy grail for all fixes for the supernatural. So many well-meaning psychics, shamans, light workers, and other people trying to be helpful constantly sing the praises of all mighty sage.

"It cleans. It clears things. It cleanses spaces of negative energy. Smudge sage around your home, and you will be fine." This advice came from many people trying to help me.

Out of desperation, I started to garner a lot of faith in the potential of these dried, crispy leaves. I went to a local metaphysical shop and bought a bundle of sage. It had some other pretty dried flowers in it, too. I asked the sales lady if this would help me clear my home.

"Oh yes. This is made especially for this store by a local shaman," she said.

"How many should I buy?" I asked her.

"These are quite powerful, so you only need one," she said.

I returned with my glorious little bundle of sage filled with high hopes. There were so many ghosts in our home that, by now, I had officially coined our place "The Ghost

Super-Highway." For some reason, our residence became magnetic to these wayward souls.

As my daughter would share with me what she observed, I would create this Dr. Seuss-style book about them in my head. "There are fat ones, hairy ones, scary ones. Tall ones, small ones. Lazy ones, hazy ones. Brown ones, red ones, not so dead ones." You get the idea. Humor can be your friend in crazy situations.

At this time in our lives, the scariest ghost seemed to be this psychotic murderer who claimed to have killed several women and then himself. He would fly around the house fast, yelling "Red Rum" repeatedly. I didn't know at first what that meant. I found out later that "Red Rum" is murder spelled backward. Just great.

The need to free my home and family from this nightmare got even more urgent. This guy made Annabelle seem tame.

When I returned home, I hastily took out this precious bundle of sage and read and reread the directions on activating its magical powers. I wanted to ensure I did this right, leaving no margin for error.

I was excited for my family to come home from school and work later that day and have them see and feel the difference. The thought of picking up my daughter from school and having her come home to a ghost-free house was the best gift I could ever give her. This would be better than any birthday present or even Christmas morning.

I started to burn the sage and walked it around the house, spreading the spicy-smelling smoke as instructed. Nothing happened.

I decided to wait to see if I could feel some sort of energetic shift. Our house had an oppressive feeling. Walking through our home, it felt like a coat of sludge. That's the only way I can describe it. The sooty film wouldn't leave and linger on all the surfaces. Anyone who has lived through this understands how hard this is to describe.-Your brain becomes fogged. You can't think clearly. Your view of objects appears to be covered in a film-like substance.

Two hours post sage smudging, I couldn't feel or sense any changes. It was time to pick up my girls from school. I hoped that by the time we all returned, these ghosts and other beings would be gone, or at least there would be less of them.

I still had some hope that a miracle would happen. I didn't tell my girls about the sage. I needed to see if they noticed any difference.

After about 15 minutes of being home, my daughter started complaining about Annabelle's antics. I was crushed. What little hope I had of solving this ghostly problem was fully extinguished. I felt like I had entered a catatonic state that paralyzed my body, and I just went to bed. It was only 4 pm, but that didn't matter because, at some point, I would be woken up by some harassing entity.

The following day, a concerned friend called me. She asked me how I was doing and said she needed to check in on me. She said she had no idea why. She was one of the few people who knew about the ghost issue we were dealing with. I told her about saging the house the day before.

"Did you use *white* sage?" she asked me.

"I didn't know there was a difference," I said. "I just bought whatever the salesperson told me to buy. She told me that some special shaman made it. But it didn't work. It didn't even make a dent in our number of ghosts."

"I am going to stop by tonight." She told me.

The fact that she was so kind and compassionate and willing to help restored my hope just a bit.

She came by later that evening with 12 neatly wrapped bundles of white sage. She told me to burn only one at a time, as they are rather powerful, and to keep the other bundles as needed for a later date.

She recommended saging all corners of the house, closets, cabinets, and even the garage. She instructed me to open a window or a door so these spirits could quickly leave. She warned me not to burn the sage at night. Too much disturbance at night could be a problem.

I complied even though I couldn't see how things could get worse.

Depending on my changing emotional state, two parallel thoughts ran through my mind. First, I didn't want this nightmare of entities to become someone else's problem. Second, I continued to search for a way out of the constant commotion that engulfed my innocent family. We desperately needed a resolution to the ongoing assault of paranormal activity.

The following day, I took the girls to school and was ready to battle.

I remembered my friend's instructions and followed them to the letter, except for one not-so-small part. She said only to burn one bundle at a time. I remembered thinking to myself, "Screw that. If one is good, then twelve will be REALLY good!" I opened the backyard sliding glass door a crack, got my largest silver mixing bowl, dumped all twelve bundles of sage into the bowl, and lit them on fire.

I clearly didn't think this through because, in an instant, the smoke detectors all went off, and the silver mixing bowl became a giant inferno with flames shooting out about a foot taller than the mixing bowl.

It immediately got too hot to hold, and I tossed it onto the dining room table. To this day, I thank God it didn't tip over. I stared in disbelief as I watched the fire grow to almost two feet tall and more. It started to singe the ceiling. Opening my front door, I grabbed a pair of hot pads and ran this bowl of saging inferno outside. Both the dog and cats darted out the back door while I hurried back inside and opened all our windows. In a fit of rage, I ripped off every smoke detector and broke them just to get them to shut up.

I went back outside, and the fire in my mixing bowl subsided as I doused it with a hose to ensure any embers wouldn't start vegetation on fire. As this happened, I noticed I could see glimpses of these ghosts and beings through the smoke for the first time.

At this point, I just hoped and prayed that none of my neighbors would call the fire department as I watched billows of smoke pouring out of the windows of my house. I couldn't return to my house because the smoke was so thick. I grabbed my car keys and drove around aimlessly for hours.

I felt like I was entirely out of options.

When I picked up my girls from school, they asked me why I smelled like smoke, and I told them what had happened. When we got home, the house was still embedded with smoke, to the point where I took them to Starbucks to do homework and then out to dinner. It took almost two full days to get the stench of smoke out of our house.

After this experience, I kept pondering, "Why sage? Why do so many people swear by this stuff? It offered no cure for our situation other than the fact that this smoke could have shortened our lifespans.

What I know about sage is that it is an astringent and can help with specific ailments, such as digestion. Dried sage has a lot of nutritional vitamins, such as Vitamin K, folate, iron, and other nutrients. How sage became the go-to solution to remove ghosts and entities is still a mystery because it does not work unless the dark side has implanted that thought within us.

After the failed sage experiment, I became more determined to save my family from the uninvited troupe of supernatural entities living in my home and haunting my little girl. But what would the solution be? The Ghostly Superhighway needed to end—now.

At this point, I'd learned a lot. But once again, I felt so far from getting much-needed help and answers.

# MEETING KIERA

Remember the kind psychic, Nancy, I mentioned previously? She told me I would meet a woman in uniform; the person who would help me climb out of the paranormal horror film my family could never seem to escape, or so I thought.

I forgot about that interaction for almost two years, until one fateful night, when a friend attended a dinner party. Seated next to a woman, the inevitable question was asked, "What do you do?" The woman answered that she was a shaman.

At the time, my family had survived all the craziness, but I was at rock bottom. One of the most important concepts I learned about the word 'survive' is that it means not to thrive. Think about this. If you are surviving, you are just hanging on, and that's it. This was the lifestyle we had grown accustomed to, and it was not healthy.

My sweet, unassuming life had become a battlefield, and it was brutal. We had been dealing with the constant parade of weirdness, and I missed my old life. I wanted my life as a schoolteacher to return; the life where I wasn't on edge waiting for the next proverbial paranormal shoe to drop.

I longed for the occasions when I could talk to my friends about anything; the days when I had no secrets. I wanted to see my daughter smile and laugh and not see horrible entities that no one else could see. I yearned for those days when she and I didn't compete for who had the darkest circles and biggest bags under our eyes.

When I wasn't blindly attempting to fight off demons and ghosts, I was searching for help. Although I had met a myriad of people who, for the most part, wanted to help me, they didn't have the knowledge or skills we needed. Good information was hard to come by in those early days, and the secret sauce still eluded me.

It was 4:00 p.m. on a Monday when the call came. It was my friend Shelly, and I went into a panic, wondering if she was alright. I was constantly on adrenaline overload and full of dread because of all the paranormal activity in our house, and now I wondered if something terrible had happened to my friend. At this point, I felt like Eeyore, full of doom, gloom, and despair.

"Hi Laura, I have a confession to make," Shelly said. "I went to a dinner party and met this woman who said she was a shaman, and, well, I told her about Annabelle. I know you didn't want me to say anything, but I've been so worried about you. I just blurted it out. She gave me her number so you could call her."

"Wow. Thanks. I appreciate that," I said. Tiredly, I scribbled down her name and number. I thanked her, and we hung up.

I stared numbly at my note for a while. I was too tired to dial the phone, let alone engage in any coherent conversation. But I thought, "What do I have to lose, other than ten minutes?"

As I dialed the number, I heard the phone ring on the other end. One, two, then three rings. Feeling defeated, I almost hung up. What was the point? Another psychic? Another letdown? Another disappointment?

"Hello?" said this happy, chipper voice on the other end of the phone.

I detested happy, chipper people. I was downright envious of them. After all, I'm an Aries, and we tend to be a pretty happy bunch. I wanted to be one of them again and had no idea how that could ever be possible.

"Hi, is this Kiera?" I asked. "My name is Laura, and you were at a dinner party and sat beside a woman named Deb. She said you could help me with an unusual problem."

"Probably. What is going on?" she asked me. This woman, whom I never met, seemed genuinely concerned about my situation.

"Well, we have a ghost in our home named Annabelle, and my daughter can see and talk to her," I told her.

I dared not tell Kiera about all the other entities haunting our home. Who would believe the stories about Prissy or the three-headed crocodile? I just wanted to keep it simple.

"I can help you with her. Do you have time right now?" she asked me.

The level of confidence and care in her voice surprised me. She was willing to help me on the spot! The energy I felt from her over the phone struck me as refreshing, inspiring, and even hopeful.

But I had been hopeful before, and I stopped believing because if I had hope and I lost it again, I would sink to a new low. Right now, I was as low as I could possibly fathom. The tone of Kiera's voice held a frequency that I couldn't quite identify, but I felt safe with this woman whom I couldn't see.

As we talked, I could see Annabelle as clear as day. Until now, I could only see her outline and feel or sense her. I had never been able to see her in full aspect before this moment. As Kiera worked to help Annabelle cross over, Annabelle looked right at me and thanked me. I was stunned. It felt so real.

A super tiny spark of hope lit up in me for the first time in what seemed like forever.

That is when Kiera asked me THE question.

"Is there anyone else you can see who needs to be crossed over?" she asked.

And that is when it happened. I could see him with my own eyes.

My faithful dad showed up right in front of my face. He had been with my family all this time, trying his best to help and protect us. Now, he was standing about six inches from my face, and he was looking at me with his giant steel blue eyes and saying something I will never, ever forget.

I realized that I was seeing my ghost dad for the first time since he died. Until this moment with Kiera, I could only sense his presence, and I relied on communication through my daughter. I felt this wasn't fair to her, but there weren't any other options. Now, not only was Annabelle visible, but so was my dad.

My dad told me he loved me and that I had a lot to learn. I could see angels with him. "I love you," I said to him.

And then, in a flash, I saw him zoom up into a momentary blinding flash of light. I was stunned. What just happened? I was speechless. Was this real? Did what I think just happened *really* happen? If this were real, if this really happened, then this would mean my dad was now in Heaven. He was no longer helping to fight our spiritual battles here on earth.

I was incredibly relieved. But also terrified.

My protector since childhood, my protector from the standpoint of being a mother fighting off dark entities, was now gone. His ghostly presence helped me so much throughout this hellish ordeal, and now it was his time to go Home. I must have been silent for a very long time.

Still trying to collect myself, I wondered how Kiera crossed over Annabelle so quickly and how suddenly I could see her and my dad in this new fashion. I was still trying to comprehend what I had just witnessed.

It left me confused yet thrilled. I felt like I regained some personal power. Perhaps I wouldn't have to rely so heavily on my psychic daughter to figure things out, which would be wonderful. Many times, I would lament about how she was cheated out of a childhood.

"Are you still there?" Kiera asked me.

"Um, yes," I muttered after clearing my throat, still stunned and at a loss for words.

"We crossed over Annabelle. Was that your dad, too?" she asked me.

How did she know that was my dad? I didn't think to ask her at the time.

"Yes. He has been living with us since his death a couple of years ago," I said, "trying to help us with Annabelle and some other bizarre happenings in our home. I know this sounds strange, but it's true."

"Do you have any questions?" she asked me.

"I . . . I don't know," I said. "I am so surprised. You have to understand; I've been looking for help for so long, and everyone who says that they can help us, well. . . haven't been able to. But this time, it felt real. I'm so exhausted I don't know what to think."

"How about you call me tomorrow?" she asked me.

"Ok." I hung up the phone and just stared at it.

Sitting at my desk, staring out the window at the evening darkness, I questioned if this was real. Reflecting upon this event, I remained awestruck, unable to fathom what lay ahead. I decided against sharing the experience with my daughter regarding crossing over her grandpa and Annabelle. I wanted to see if she noticed if they were still in our house, still haunting us.

I decided that I would call Kiera in the morning.

That night, my daughter and I slept the entire night for the first time in at least a year. At first, the ability to sleep left my daughter and me even more exhausted than *not* sleeping. We were suffering from stacked fatigue, what happens when one is so chronically tired, the body collapses. It felt too good to be true.

Hope began to feel tangible and attainable, at least for the moment.

The following day, I called Kiera, and we had a long discussion. I confessed to her about the other ghosts, Prissy, and the three-headed crocodile.

I know she thought I was a hot mess, and well, frankly, I was. She asked me if I would like to have a visit at her home so we could meet in person. She was willing to share some helpful ideas with me.

I didn't know who this person was, where she lived, or her background, but something inside told me I had to meet her. My intuition was screaming at me to see her, but I also had a slight niggle of a pause that I ignored.

I was excited to meet Kiera. Since my original call with her, my daughter has ceased complaining about Annabelle's antics. She could now take a shower without being stabbed in the back with an etheric knife, so I knew something had shifted and moved us into a better place.

Kiera was anxious to hear more about what had been happening in our home. She seemed genuinely concerned about my family. For the first time, I felt safe telling an outsider about the paranormal hell we had been going through.

As I spilled my guts about the assorted, non-corporeal characters who roamed our house, I began to cry, a flood of bottled-up emotions that had been kept at bay for far too long. There was Prissy, the hat man who would stand in the corner of the room, the three-headed crocodile who terrorized our animals, and the many other ghosts who failed to cross over, haunting us daily.

I told Kiera about the years of sleepless nights and seeking out religious and psychic professionals for assistance. Everything I experienced for the past two years came gushing out. Did it even make sense? It was as though a pressure cooker valve had popped. I felt sorry for her and wondered if she regretted inviting me over.

She was polite and listened the entire time. She shared with me some of her experiences that were similar, and I was relieved to hear someone else's stories. Suddenly, I didn't feel so alone in the world anymore. Here she was, opening her home to me...a complete stranger. As we talked, I kept glancing at the books on the shelves, realizing that Kiera knew what she was talking about.

She asked me if I could come back the following week, and she would help me start putting together a plan to handle on my situation. Kiera had been so successful on that fateful first phone call that I felt I had nothing to lose with a return visit to her home.

For the first time in a very long while, I felt my family and I were in a much safer place. I also discovered that my abilities were expanding rapidly, and could now see the same paranormal activities as my daughter and more. My dormant childhood abilities were now returning stronger than ever. It gave me great relief to take some of that burden off my daughter so that she could live a normal childhood.

Each week for about two months, I went to Kiera's house, collected my glass of iced tea, and discussed the paranormal world. This became our everyday world, and it was such a blessing to hear how logically another person dealt with the same experiences.

One day, as I was sitting in her living room contemplating the concept of our destiny when I saw it—the picture of a woman in uniform—sitting right there in front of me the entire time.

I looked at her and said, "Oh my gosh. You are the woman in uniform I was told I would meet. I completely forgot about what Nancy, the psychic, had told me almost two years ago."

Reflecting on how karma works, I have had many epiphanies over the years. Many of my learning experiences have been about what works, what doesn't, and why. Looking back, had I not met Kiera at the beginning of this paranormal upheaval, I would not have appreciated all those lessons I needed to learn.

I spent nearly five years in my association with Kiera, and I am grateful for what I learned. She was an amazing teacher and guide. Kiera also learned a lot from me during that time, and we mostly worked well together. As strong women, we learned to keep our egos in check, a vital component when performing spiritual services. I learned that I can't control the evil that comes our way, nor can I control people's actions. I learned to hand everything over to GodSource and to remove self-validation from our successes. Like most relationships, people come into our lives and leave when it's time. Kiera will always be a person who will remain in my memory as a source of knowledge and contemplation.

As author Brian A. "Drew" Chalker wisely said, "People come into your life for a reason, a season, or a lifetime."

# A DIFFERENT KIND OF HAUNTING

My encounter with Kiera's cousin was a massive opportunity for me to learn about how a living person could psychically attack another. It started small, and I absolutely could not fathom how a stranger could have it out for me. But then again, as a friend reminds me, karma doesn't waste energy.

It began when I started waking up with these odd bite marks and pairs of pinpricks on my body that looked like they could be from a tiny vampire. I didn't know what they were from or how they got there; all I knew was that they were consistently all over my body, night after night.

I also realized my dreams were not *my* dreams anymore. I recall hearing this constant electronic-sounding laughter, and later, it escalated into Harry Potter Dementor-style beings swirling around me. It got so bad that I stopped sleeping again, and I began to dread nightfall.

Often, I would end up in my living room trying to evade sleep and fight these nightmarish beings. Wishing, hoping, praying, and begging for guidance was now an hourly request that seemed to fall on deaf ears over the course of the next couple of years.

The torture was endless, and it escalated into the daytime hours.

At times, I would be home alone working on my computer when suddenly, something dark and heavy would come up from behind and start choking me. It would grab me at the lower part of my throat in the soft tissue, right above the cervical bone. I could feel three distinct fingers that pressed harder and harder. The first few times, I didn't know what to do; I was in shock. I *thought* I was home alone.

After a while, I started exerting my authority over this unseen entity. I demanded it leave my home and brought in spiritual reinforcements. As I learned to gather my spiritual strength and stamina, this entity also grew in power.

One afternoon, I found myself passed out from being choked. About a minute later, when I awoke, I found my hands behind my back as if they were energetically tied together. I had been sitting at my computer with my hands in front of me. How did my hands get put behind my back?

Another instance occurred on a beautiful summer day when I went to the local Trader Joe's grocery store alone. I parked the car, got out, and walked about 50 feet when I was suddenly pushed from behind so hard that I ended up falling face-first and karate-chopping the curb in front of me, breaking my hand. No one was near enough to push me, yet several people who witnessed the occurrence were as stunned as I was.

"Wow, it looked like someone pushed you from behind," one man said. Another said he felt a huge swish of air go past him. Two others were laughing nervously, and one woman ran away. Not a single person reached out to help me. I suspect their subconscious mind was freaked out by the demon assaulting me, and I sat on the curb alone, feeling nauseated and trying not to vomit.

The battles at night had turned into battles during the day and continued for years. Finally, one night, the truth revealed itself, but not how I imagined. None other than Jesus presented himself to me.

He said, "You are the devil. You deserve all of this, and I will not stop until you are destroyed." To say I was shocked would be an understatement.

Then, this figure standing in front of me began hurling "hot bombs." I have no other words to describe it, and they left burn marks on my skin. Studying the apparition, I realized Jesus didn't *feel* like Jesus. Something was off; not quite right.

Coming to my senses, I immediately ran a volcano of salt through him, and that's when I saw Kiera's cousin for an ultra-brief moment. Then it was gone. I realized this being was a shapeshifter, somehow related to Kiera's cousin.

At the time, I didn't understand the hows and whys of what I was experiencing. And then I learned why. Kiera's cousin and I had at least one past life together that didn't go well. A couple of weeks later, sitting in my acupuncturist's waiting room, a spontaneous past life recollection came flooding over me. It was incredibly vivid.

In this past life, I was a top European seamstress, I believe in France, and Kiera's cousin worked for me. She was jealous and wanted my life. She wanted my husband and baby girl. In the vision, I was wearing a green dress when she came up from behind and choked me to death, pretending to find my body. After my death, she married my husband and became my daughter's mother. What's even more interesting is that, to this day, I hate sewing. In fact, I barely passed sewing class in middle school, and perhaps it was a muscle memory recall.

While this vision was happening, I began being physically choked at the acupuncturist's office, to the point where I was gagging and gasping for air, except no one was in the room with me. The acupuncturist walked in and saw me being choked, but not by a physical person. As a psychic herself who got "impressions," she confirmed all that I already knew.

That is when I realized that this cousin's subconscious viewed me as a threat, and this validation was instrumental for me to frame the situation and remind myself that I wasn't losing my mind with these psychic assaults. I also discovered that her spiritual team was tasked with torturing and eliminating me. I didn't know why at the time, but now it all made sense.

The prolonged torture left me relatively well-educated about how the dark side works. We all have spiritual teams, which is our soul tribe. It's important to note that not all spiritual teams come from the light. Some come from the dark. This was a monumental "aha" moment for me.

The question became one of, "How do you return the energy from a living person who is haunting you? What is the role of free will?"

We have the right to defend ourselves in all dimensions. I had to learn how to protect myself within the confines of spiritual law. It was a challenging lesson, especially during a time when people avoided discussions about these topics in a public format. Fortunately, things have changed, and we can discuss these issues freely and without backlash.

When I learned that the living could haunt the living, it changed everything. In most scenarios, when we think of hauntings, we think of the dead haunting the living. This isn't always the case, and understanding this helped me expand my gifts on a whole new level. In addition, I also learned that we all have spirit guides, but not all guides are from the higher realms. It's a big topic, and we'll explore that more later.

# REPTILIAN HELL BREAKS LOOSE

I had about a two-month reprieve from the dark side; the hauntings, the torture, and the interrupted sleep seemed to be distant memories. The animals in our home were relaxed, and my family was happy and not chronically tired. I was gaining the upper hand in all this paranormal craziness—or so I thought.

One evening, a new form of hell broke out in our house at an entirely new level. I found out later that the local middle school had brought in a guest speaker: a survivor of the Nazi concentration camps. She had an important message to impart to our youth: Never forget.

And this is where I learned about the entanglement between the dark side and the dead. I was in the hallway when I felt some sort of whip mark on my ankles. Then, in an instant, there were many constant whip marks and welts showing up on my ankles and lower legs.

I was taken aback by what I saw pouring into one of my daughter's dressing mirrors. Hundreds, if not thousands, of Nazi concentration camp victims came pouring in, looking for safety. They told me they broke free and were running from the Nazis. I was stunned. What the heck? How does this work, and how did they find me? I was able to speak to one of the ghost victims, who said they followed my daughter home so they could find me.

Then I realized where those whip marks were coming from. The Nazis. Only these Nazis were not former humans. They were not ghosts. They were reptilians. There were hundreds of them, and they were all running around my home, trying to recapture the escapees.

I immediately created a containment field for the victims in the street. One element I learned is it's best not to help or do this work in the same space where I am physically located. Why? Because they can cause me harm, intentionally or unintentionally.

I started to cross over the victims of the Nazis. This ticked off the reptilians, which meant they no longer had control over those souls. The reptilians cannot enter that containment field because it's a frequency issue. Yes, these concentration camp victims had been soul-napped in death—a very horrifying piece of information.

The reptilians had captured them in death, and they were all still being tortured. My big lesson was that death isn't an automatic pass to Heaven, no matter your faith, karma, or belief structure.

These dark entities can soul-nap us. It's a violation of spiritual law, and they don't care. What is important to note is that frequencies can create a barrier.

And yes, I was able to remove those reptilians permanently.

# WHO'S WHO IN
# THE SPIRITUAL ZOO?

W hen we embark on a path of studying spirituality, there
is much information—some good, some not so good.
But I have found that most books and teachings only focus
on the light side: with enough love, light, and hope, one can
thwart even the vilest of dark entities.

This is a problem. This is what the dark side wants us to
do. It keeps us vulnerable and weak, cloaks us from certain
realities, prevents us from searching for more effective tools
to deal with the dark side, prevents us from learning, and, in
the end, caps our spiritual growth. We need to understand the
dark side to better understand the light side. Karma always
seeks balance.

Think about it this way: before the invention of the microscope, people didn't believe that viruses and bacteria existed
because we couldn't see them with the naked eye. With the
microscope, a whole new world unfolded before us. The
more we learned how viruses and bacteria worked, the safer
and healthier we became. We knew that washing our hands
saved lives.

Let's consider this concept when studying how the dark side works. After all, knowledge is power.

Discerning who's who and in what dimension is essential. As humans, we tend to classify and organize the world around us. We do this to create order. It also grounds and helps us to learn about our surrounding environments. Why shouldn't this apply in other dimensions?

For instance, on the surface, a rattlesnake and a garden snake are both snakes, right? If we further classify these two snakes, we find out that one can be deadly, and one can be helpful. But they are both snakes.

Think about the last time you were at a zoo. Imagine yourself in a section and you can see lions, tigers, elephants, and meerkats. Then someone walks up to you and says, "Hey, look at that mammal!" How do you know which mammal they are talking about?

When we are sensitive enough to see, feel, or sense energies in another dimension, the ability to learn discernment will keep us safe.

# THE THIRD DIMENSION: BOOTS ON THE GROUND

This is the dimension in which we are currently living. This is our physical, mortal world. This is where we use our senses of sight, hearing, touch, smell, and taste in the tangible world. The third dimension is the place where you are reading this book right now: your living room recliner, lying in bed, or on a long bus commute.

The physical body we are born with merely serves as a cloak for what lies beneath – our soul—the personality, intuition, and the energetic love that pulses in and out of our hearts.

This is the dimension into which our souls incarnate and reincarnate. We return here within our soul or family groups for the lessons and experiences we need on our karmic path for our soul's (hopefully) evolution.

It's important to realize that our souls are eternal, and our physical bodies are only used for this incarnation. However, the physical bodies we incarnate into are based on our karma and our soul's particular needs for those lessons, experiences, soul purposes, and possibly a soul mission.

It doesn't mean that someone who gets cancer or has a life-changing accident *deserves* that. It *might* be that those around that person need to have the experiences of caring for someone else and learning greater depths of compassion and love.

The same is true for a child born with some disability or anomaly. It's a karmic opportunity that offers us many rich experiences. Could it be that a child born with a disability is there to help his family spiritually by providing the experiences they need for their soul evolution? By caring for that specific child and their unique needs, they will hopefully learn what unconditional love is.

Once, during fall break, I took my girls to a trampoline gym with a friend and her daughters. The girls were off playing and having a good time when I noticed this mom who had brought her son, who had cerebral palsy, to the gym. This mom was so loving and devoted to her son.

I couldn't help myself with this voyeurism, knowing that her son wouldn't be able to experience what my daughters could. I continued to watch them over the next few minutes. This mom would never be able to send her son off to college by himself or see him walk down the aisle with his bride. She would never see him grow up and be fully independent.

At first, it left me feeling a bit sad for her. But I realized those life events probably didn't matter to her. She loved every day and every challenge she would have with him. I am sure many of her days were difficult, but that can be said for every parent. I learned a lot in those few moments of watching their interactions. Perhaps this mom and her son were my karmic opportunity so that I could learn.

This is what life in the third dimension is all about. Earth is a fantastic schoolhouse and an opportunity for learning and growth. The best part is that we get to come back over and over, right?

This third-dimensional realm requires a few specific ingredients: time, space, and gravity. We need the time to have these experiences our souls need, the space to carry out our mortal lives, and the gravity to anchor us in that time and space. It's all called the human experience.

Mortal man has been given free will. This is an important concept to understand as we move forward. Free will means we can make choices. Every decision we make earns us karma.

Karma, in its most basic form, is simply action and reaction. It's also called the law of consequences. You get angry and kick something hard, and you end up causing yourself pain and possibly breaking a bone.

Karma is not fatalistic or predetermined. It is our ability to create and change our circumstances based on the actions and environments that we experience. Karma spans our soul's entire existence and may not be satisfied in one lifetime. Karma is not emotional, judgmental, or vengeful. It is simply balanced.

Every decision we make earns us karma, which echoes out, and this applies to the good, the bad, and the ugly.

## When Your Boss Is a Karmic Tool

How many of us have had the world's worst boss? I sure have.

I have learned that bad bosses offer us karmic opportunities to rise to the occasion, and sometimes that means getting a new job.

Let's use a generic example of a boss many of us have had. Let's say his name is Joe. Joe is demeaning to those who report to him. He especially likes to zero in on a person he views as weak and incapable. He will pit people against each other for the sheer delight in it. He's a narcissistic energy vampire. The whole workplace becomes more toxic over time.

The toxic energy of this workplace gets embedded in the people who work there. It can't be helped. You walk into a meeting, and the tension is so thick you can cut it with a knife. You find you need your weekends to heal from the toxicity of the workplace. Then Monday rolls around, and you get beaten up again.

You become exhausted and start to bring that toxic energy home because it sticks to you. You lash out at your roommate, significant other, or child. This boss is karmically responsible for what happens in the workplace, and yet, you are also karmically accountable for your actions and reactions with him, your co-workers, and your loved ones.

Many times, stepping back and observing the situation from a distance can help us gain clarity and make better free will choices.

We must remember that the third dimension is the dimension where our souls reincarnate into our physical bodies. In each reincarnation, we get a new physical body or a rental unit. This new body is an opportunity for a do-over to learn those lessons and have those experiences to help us on our karmic paths.

# THE 4TH DIMENSION:
## PURGATORY, RECONCILIATION
## OR HELL?

S ome groups call it purgatory, the hells, limbo, the lower astral. It can go by many names.

But when it's our time to 'go' and we leave our physical body, the energy that animates the body—our soul—has to go somewhere. The first law of thermodynamics states that energy is neither created nor destroyed. We also need to understand that everything is energy. The beauty of energy is that it can be transformed or transferred from one form to another.

Water is a perfect third-dimensional example of how energy works. This concept can be applied in all dimensions. Liquid water is wet and fluid. However, when the temperature of the water changes, its energy shifts. When water is at 0 degrees Celsius or 32 degrees Fahrenheit, it becomes solid. Why? Because the molecules of $H_2O$ become farther apart and move more slowly, it's still $H_2O$. The density of the water has changed, which is why ice will float.

When the conditions are right, water can also become a gas. Water vapor is around us all the time. When you boil water into a tea kettle, you see steam. That steam is still $H_2O$. But the water molecules are closer together and move faster. (I have a degree in science in education, but I only ever got to teach sex education. So, explaining this is fun for me.☺)

The point is that when it comes to our souls, the energy that animates the body has to go somewhere when we leave the physical body.

So, where does that energy go?

It goes to the 4th dimension. Why does this happen? The original intention of the 4th dimension was to be a step-up transformer for when our souls leave our physical bodies so that we can acclimate to the higher dimensions of the Heaven World, Heaven, Source, or Creator. You get the idea.

The energy that animates from our physical body must go somewhere when we die, which is the 4th dimension. The trick is not to stay there. Ideally, when we die, we go to the 4th dimension, see the light, and cross over into the next dimension, the 5th dimension or higher.

Consider you are on an airplane flying from San Diego to Paris. However, the trip is not a straight shot because the airplane must stop in New York City to refuel. The New York City location is like the 4th dimension in that our souls need refueling to complete our journey to heaven or, in this analogy, arrival in Paris.

What would happen if there was no fuel? You would be stuck in New York City. This analogy is essential to understand what comes next: The Lucifer Rebellion.

When Lucifer fell, he and his people had to leave the light of the Heaven World, which is a higher dimension than the 4<sup>th</sup> dimension. They no longer had access to the light of the Divine, of the Heavens. This was a problem because light is also an energy form that feeds souls that reside in Heaven.

These entities realized they needed more of that rich and sustainable Divine energy. This was a problem. Banished from the higher realms, they realized they had to go to a place where they could access an energy source.

Where did they go?

Lucifer and his clan set up shop in the 4<sup>th</sup> dimension. This would be a step-down transformer for these former beings of light. Remember, this is also the same dimension that we mortals go to on our way back Home. But getting Home is more challenging now.

Many holy texts published have some concept of the 23<sup>rd</sup> Psalm for a reason. These are a few lines that carry a lot of meaning.

"Yea, though I walk through the valley of the shadow of death, I will fear no evil."

"He Restoreth my soul; he leadeth me in the paths of righteousness."

Are these passages designed to help us cross over to receive healing for our souls? Is the valley of the shadow of death the 4<sup>th</sup> dimension, the place where evil lurks?

There are many beings and entities that now reside in the 4<sup>th</sup> dimension. The Luciferic population has grown and been left unchecked for many millennia. These beings have been in control of the 4<sup>th</sup> dimension, dramatically impacting us mortals trying to return Home.

This is why we have ghosts.

## Discernment

Often, people feel guilty or don't want to offend their spirit guides, angels, or other potential light beings with whom they communicate. When we start to perform practices or use tools to discern who or what we are connecting to, it keeps us in a much safer space. Do NOT be afraid of offending your spiritual team. When you do this, your spiritual team will be grateful to you.

One of the easiest and most effective tools we can use is salt. Salt cleanses in all dimensions. As you connect to your spiritual team through prayer, meditation, or any other manner, visualize yourself pouring a rain of salt over them. If they remain, then chances are pretty good that this is the spiritual team that is for your greater good.

If they disappear, don't feel bad. Be grateful. You dodged a bullet.

I remember a client of mine whose mother had died. She asked me to help her to cross her over. My client had a teenage daughter who was devastated by the loss of her grandma. Her teenager was psychic. My client's daughter had two friends who told her she could summon grandma with an Ouija board. And that is what they did- or they thought they did. My friend's daughter was so excited to talk to her 'crossed over' grandma that she told her mom what she did.

The client called me and asked how this could have happened. I asked if I could come over to her house to find out what had happened.

When I got to the house, we sat down in the living room, and I asked the daughter to request that 'grandma' come. The granddaughter was so proud and excited to do this. Once 'Grandma' was summoned, I poured etheric salt, a visualization technique, all over 'Grandma,' and she shape-shifted into a nasty wraith with scales and red and yellow eyes.

When I used salt, it could no longer hold that form of the grandma, and it was exposed. I properly removed this entity because it's important to make sure this entity and its friends don't become someone else's problem. Then, I requested my spiritual team to remove this entity.

## Characters in the Play

One of the most emotionally complex concepts is that not just ghosts reside in the fourth dimension. Luciferic forces have taken over this dimension, which is where the Cabal/Satanic concepts originated. Many types of beings live in this realm, and they all need an energy or fuel source.

One of the most accessible energy sources is ghosts. Why? Because they are of the light. Our soul essences come from God. This light is an energy source that all beings and entities need to sustain themselves. When the Luciferic forces left the light of God, they needed to find another energy source. The logical place is the 4th dimension.

It's essential to understand how this dimension works. Knowledge is power. The ability to know and understand these concepts diminishes the fears we may have towards them. It takes away their ability to harm. These dark 4th-dimensional beings significantly impact our mortal lives and not for our greater good.

If you can see or sense beings in other dimensions, it's imperative not to blindly trust who or what you *think* you are communicating with is who or what they say they are. The beings in the 4<sup>th</sup> dimension can fool anyone at any time. This concept also holds true in our physical, third-dimensional world. How many times have we read that some beloved priest, soccer coach, or trusted confidant ended up being a pedophile?

This is why tools of discernment are critical in all dimensions. Trust your intuition. If you have difficulty trusting your intuition, give yourself the gift of learning how to develop it. See section three for more information on developing your intuition.

The following is a short, general list of beings that reside in the 4<sup>th</sup> dimension.

**Greys:** Greys are extraterrestrials and interdimensional beings, meaning they can transcend time and space. They use specialized technology to phase in and out of physical bodies on the Earth plane. Encounters with Greys are generally not for the betterment of humanity. They have a hive-mind mentality and are interconnected through their technologies. They like to experiment on humans and animals.

**Reptilians:** Reptilians are one of many alien entities influencing many of us. In a nutshell, the reptilians are the ones who created the Communist form of government we see on our planet. They utilize humans as worker bees. They will infiltrate governments and inhabit our global leaders. If you are sensitive enough to see between the dimensions, look at some of our global leaders, and you may see some physical anomalies.

They can come and go into humans. As they do this, they take over that human's soul. In essence, they kidnap the soul. We often think of the concept of a kidnapping as purely third-dimensional. This is why creating a healthy and strong soul is vital to our soul sovereignty. They cannot access us when our soul is strong. As a side note, the Greys are also responsible for our capitalistic societies of debits and credits.

A while back, I was speaking at an event where another speaker was a channeler. Please be wary of channelers. The light side doesn't need to enter your body to give you information. This channeler brought in a reptilian. Oh, I was on high alert with this one.

I could see the reptilian overlay on the speaker. This reptilian was telling the crowd that they were responsible for the start of WWII and that humanity needed to rise and ascend. I looked around, and the entire room was in a trance, with bowed heads. This being had control over them. That is when I started to ask this reptilian a question. "How does starting a world war help humanity," I asked. The next thing I knew, this demon stood up and stared at me. Then I felt wrapping tethers around my arms and legs. I broke them off and left the event.

**The Hat Man**: This universal entity took up residence in my daughter's bedroom. It was there 24/7. It never talked, never moved. The evil that it exuded was terrifying. I don't know his purpose other than to observe and collect data. To this day, I can't stand the sight of a fedora.

**Lower realms:** These tend to be the shadowy specters that many of us can see out of the corner of our eyes. They are more like harasser beings. They thrive off of negative emotional states and behaviors. The more emotional and behavioral turmoil available, the more they feast. They can also attach themselves to the living.

**Black magicians**: These guys are a dime a dozen and tend to be fragile and power-hungry. There is a political hierarchy with them as well because politics exists in all dimensions. These guys like to have control over other dark entities like lower realms and then have them do their bidding.

**Shapeshifters:** These entities love to disguise themselves as other beings, perhaps Jesus, your grandma, or anything in between. They can read our minds and even put dark thoughts in our heads. When we are aware of this, we become better able to consciously break the ties to them because it creates an innate awareness of when our thoughts may not be our own.

There is a documentary on Amazon called "Beware of Angels." It talks about a Sunday school group that started channeling angels. By no coincidence, this happened about 50 miles from where I now live. This group let their egos get in the way, and some bad things happened. They were so excited about the exclusivity of connecting to these 'higher' realm beings, and they didn't use discernment when connecting to them. They unquestioningly believed that these beings were for their greater good. This documentary is an excellent example of how persistent these dark ones are.

Other types of beings reside in the 4th dimension, but here are the main players:

**Thought forms:** We need first to understand that everything is energy. This includes our thoughts. There is a phrase by Prentice Mulford that holds true, "Thoughts are things." This concept applies in all dimensions. For years, our home was plagued by this three-headed crocodile. It was created by one of the dark entities that terrorized us. Once Kiera had told me to salt this little bugger, it disappeared. It came back a few times, but I always salted it. This thought form would roam the house and terrorize our family pets. My daughter could see it, and I couldn't. But I always knew it was around when our perfectly house-trained rabbit would start madly thumping his foot against our wood floors.

**Ghosts:** What is a ghost? A ghost is simply a soul stuck between heaven and earth. They reside in the 4th dimension. The concepts of ghosts, angels, and demons span the history of this planet, crossing cultures and languages—for example, fifth-century B.C. India has words and concepts for these entities, as does 12th-century A.D. Ireland and the 20th-century United States.

If they don't exist, how can this be?

A ghost is a former human without the physical shell of a body. This former human is somebody's loved one, a child, mother, cousin, uncle, friend. A ghost should never, ever be a novelty act for profit. It's unkind and lacks compassion, and let's not even get into the karma of this.

There are so many haunted places that monetize those poor souls who are stuck in limbo. Haunted tours are offered worldwide for a few thrill-seeking moments that capitalize on someone's misfortune. Where is the spiritual service when it comes to this type of ghost hunting?

If you had a child who died, would you want this for your child? Or would you want your child to be afforded that ability to go Home? Would you like your loved one's soul to be paraded around like some circus freak show? Of course not. You would want to help them to go Home.

# THE FIFTH DIMENSION:
# HEAVEN BY ANOTHER NAME

For the purposes of this book, we need to focus on the 5$^{th}$ dimension and the higher realms as a generality. This 5$^{th}$ dimension goes by many names. The Higher Realms, Heaven, Heaven World, Source, Home, the Light, Light Source, God Source, and Isle of Paradise are some of the more familiar names.

This is where higher frequency Divine beings reside, such as Counselors of Divine Wisdom, The Ancients of Days, Lord Babaji, angels, and other beings of the light. These beings do not reside in the 4$^{th}$ dimension. Why? Because it's a frequency issue.

The frequency of these dimensions is much higher than the 4$^{th}$ dimension. I used to be a math teacher, and I realized that math is the key. It's about frequency. The more we study, learn, and apply wisdom, the more we can raise our frequency. The higher we can raise our frequency, the more we connect to God, the Divine Source.

Angels are an essential aspect of humanity because they are here to serve, assist, and guide us. They are also messengers, here to help us mortals. Angels are not a religious dogma. The abiding characteristic about angels is they don't have free will as we humans do. Angels are here to assist us and can only do so within the confines of spiritual law.

That means they cannot interfere with or violate our free will. They cannot act on our behalf unless we request their assistance. We need to ASK them for help. But we need to be specific and timely and make sure our requests for help don't violate another person's free will. Remember the popular TV show *Star Trek*? At all costs, the crew of the starship Enterprise were not allowed to interfere with other worlds they visited because adhering to the Prime Directive was paramount to their mission. It's the same with angels.

What does infringe upon another person's free will look like?

It has many forms. If my cousin is a drug addict and I want him to get clean, I can't request an angel to clean him up, help him stop using drugs, or make him better. He must want this for himself even though you love your cousin, and you see how his destructive behaviors affect him and the entire family. Why can't I do that? Because the cousin has free will. The free will to make choices. This is his karmic path. They are his experiences and consequences, no matter how much you want to help him.

What you can do is this: let's say you are going to a family event, and you know your drug-addict cousin will be there. You can ask for a team of angels from Heaven World to accompany you to the family event for the entire get-together. What this will do is help protect you, and it will bring your cousin into the frequency of angels for a bit of time.

It may help him in the long term, but it may not. But the point is you are not violating his free will. However, when you put yourself in the presence of angels, that action may be uplifting for those around you.

We can ask angels to help guide us in making wise decisions. We can ask angels to accompany us into a heated business meeting or when talking with a manipulative person so that we may choose wiser words and react more thoughtfully.

We can't request that an angel impose on another person's free will on our behalf. For instance, I can't make an angel stop my loved one from being a drug addict. I also can't request an angel to make someone love me or get my dream job.

The most important aspect about angels is that we all have access to them. But we must remember that we have to ask for their help and guidance. Angels can be the basis of anyone's spiritual team if we choose to enlist their help and guidance.

One more tip on angels: Angels earn karma when we request their assistance. This means that asking them for help helps those angels on their souls' path. Don't be afraid to impose on them; you are not bothering them. You deserve to ask for their help and guidance.

When we make this a regular practice, it helps us in all aspects of our lives. It can raise our frequency because we are directly connecting to the Divine. It can prevent us from having knee-jerk reactions to challenging situations and help us attain wisdom. Angels are so important because each time we request their assistance, they connect us to the Divine and higher realms. They are compassionate and benevolent beings.

Yes, *you* do deserve that!

Many other types of light beings are here to help and serve humanity.

**Pleiadians:** These benevolent humanoid extraterrestrials strive to offset some of the nefarious alien agendas.

**Arcturians:** they are compassionate and benevolent beings who are here to assist humanity with ascension and spiritual growth.

**Sirians:** They are considered to be guardians and helpers

**Lyrans:** Lyrans are protectors and spiritual warriors.

All these beings and more are considered part of several galactic foundations. This means that we do have help. We do have hope.

# WHAT DOES YOUR SPIRITUAL TEAM LOOK LIKE?

As mortals, spiritual beings spending some time in physical bodies, we need to understand we are never alone. We all have spiritual teams. But here's the deal: not all teams play for the same side.

Think about that for a moment. Every soul has a spiritual team. Some play for the light side, some for the dark side, and there is a lot of gray in between. Our spiritual teams change based on our frequency and levels of spiritual service. It's essential to understand this.

We will not always have the same spiritual team members in this life or our previous or future incarnations. There is a saying that the only constant in life is change, including our spiritual teams.

Let's break this down a bit. We all have a spiritual team, and our teams vary in size. Some people may have a small, tight-knit team. Others may have a larger team. Our teams may contain other beings than just angels. It's not a judgment call. It just is.

However, we need to recognize that our teams are *earned*. How do we earn our teams? The answer is through our deeds or actions of spiritual service, or lack thereof. Spiritual service comes in many forms; often, it's not some grandiose action. It can be as simple as helping an elderly person across the street or a politician who works for the betterment of her community. Perhaps a schoolteacher who takes an extra moment with a hurting child or even the simple act of picking up a piece of trash.

These types of acts are all positive forms of spiritual service.

Spirituality is a harmonic scale with ups and downs, ebbs and flows. It is never, ever a straight shot up. This is because mortal life throws all sorts of challenges at us. An unexpected death, job loss, divorce, and unwanted pregnancy. It happens, but these challenges offer us a myriad of opportunities.

It's essential to recognize that everyone has a spiritual path, and it is not up to us to judge where we may *think* someone else is on their path. We need to understand that we are all here for the experiences and lessons that are unique to each of us.

The higher realms have many layers and levels, and the bottom line is that each time we connect with our angels in the higher realms, we connect to God, Source, or whatever name we choose. Our service on this planet is all about making the world a better place.

# REASONS WHY A SOUL
# MAY NOT CROSS OVER

## Unfinished Business

We have been conditioned over millennia to explain why a ghostly soul may not have crossed over. One of the biggest is "they have unfinished business."

Of course, they do.

When a soul dies in an accident, violent death, or what they deem too soon, they may think they have unfinished business, but sometimes business gets cut short. However, when you exit your physical body, your time here on this planet is done -- for now. Typically, a ghost cannot make banking transactions or change the diaper of their young child.

## Might Not Know They Have Died

If a person is suddenly ejected out of their body, they may not know they are dead, just like Annabelle and Emily from section one.

I first realized this was an issue when the Japanese tsunami hit in 2011. All of a sudden, my home was filled with angry Japanese ghost men and crying children who couldn't find their moms and dads and a few other body-less souls. At the time, I couldn't understand how they found us. Japan is not close to California.

But somehow, they all saw this light that they were attracted to and found us. It was devastating news around the globe at the time. My family and I were talking and thinking about all those poor people who were affected by this tragic event. None of them knew they had died. They were walking down the street, talking on the phone, heading to school, and then bam, their mortal life was over.

## Looking for an Adult in Charge

Children often become stuck between dimensions because they are used to looking for an adult in charge. If they don't know to go to the light, it could fade away before the child reaches it. If the parents are grieving so hard that they can't let go, the child becomes trapped between Heaven and Earth. It's not that the parents were malicious. Their grief may have been too much. Losing a child is not the natural order . . . or so we think.

I remember taking my child to the doctor for a check-up. While we were there, Joey, a child ghost, entered the room. This eight-year-old ghost child was dressed in a hospital gown with tubes still attached. He told me he had died from an operation and he didn't know what to do. He had been following his doctor around, hoping the doctor could help him. He loved his doctor and looked up to him, but he couldn't understand why the doctor didn't know he was there.

This little boy said he saw a bright light when he died, and he wasn't sure he should go to it because no one was around to tell him what he should do. What a dilemma! I told the boy that since he saw us, I would cross him over right then. He smiled and thanked me as he was sandwiched between two angels.

## Sometimes, the Dead Want to Punish the Living

If you are a jerk in life, chances are you will be a jerk in death. Sometimes, the dead want to haunt the living to punish the living person for whatever reason. This is not good karma, and it is not suitable for their soul's evolution. Crossing over this personality type helps them and improves your karma.

Years ago, I had one of those "karmic tools" of a boss. This person delighted in torturing others, and he loved his position of superiority within his staff. One day, we found out that his sister had died. Within a month of the passing of his sister, my boss started to get intense backaches and had to stop coming into the office. He had been out of the office for a few weeks and then returned. When he returned, I could clearly see the ghost of his sister beating him over and over on his back and his head. The living boss had no idea his sister was haunting him.

I looked at this ghost, astonished. I had never seen a ghost beat on a living person to that degree. I asked her why she was doing this. She told me that she spent her entire childhood being beaten by her older brother and that it was payback time. Her rage against her brother was so intense that I can still recall it.

I learned a lot from my former boss' ghostly sister. Because this ghost was in my space, it gave me the spiritual jurisdiction to cross her over. I acknowledged that, yes, he had done terrible things to her. I explained to this ghost that she was incurring negative karma by beating him and not crossing over. She didn't care about that. But since she was in my space, I had the authority to cross her over and send her Home.

Within days of crossing her over, my boss' backache ceased, and he returned to the office. He never knew what happened; it wasn't mine to tell, though I wanted to. This boss seemed to have a lot to learn about treating people, which stemmed from his childhood. Chances are this boss, who beat his sister, will be a jerk in death.

I hope when his time comes, he crosses over.

## Sometimes, the Living Inadvertently Haunt the Dead

When a loved one appears to die too soon, the family may be holding onto them so tightly they can't let them go, even if that soul wants to cross over. I have seen these etheric tentacles strapped to a ghost that the living inadvertently created so that the soul cannot leave and becomes trapped between dimensions.

I remember one of my daughters had a friend who lost her mom to brain cancer. I had been at this family's house several times, picking up and dropping off kids. I knew that the ghost mom was in their house. I knew she had died and not crossed over. But I couldn't help her.

The dad told me he knew she was still in the house, and it comforted him to know she was still there. He did love her, but his love for her was limited. What does this mean? I could have crossed her over. However, without his permission, I had no spiritual jurisdiction to cross her over. This was his house. The law is the same as it is in our physical world. I could not cross her over in his home more than I could walk out the door with their computer.

One day, my daughter's friend came over to our house. I couldn't believe it. The ghost mom came with her. Let me tell you, she was angry at her family. Her rage was intense. At the time, I was trying to get some snacks together for the kids before their soccer practice when this ghost mom grabbed me by the throat and choked me. Hard. I was stunned.

I left the kitchen and went to my bedroom to have some privacy. She told me she could see my light and felt I could help her. She spent months trying to leave her house so I could help her. Somehow, she became bound to the location of the house. I had no idea why. I knew she was a ghost in her home, but I also knew I could do nothing to help her without permission. Once she could leave her house with her daughter and enter my home, I had the spiritual jurisdiction to help her.

She said that her husband knew she was in the house, and she was so angry at him for keeping her a prisoner. I'll never forget her statement to me. She explained she was still in the same pain from the cancers that ended her life and what her family was doing to her was cruel and unusual punishment.

"I was a good wife and mother. Why did they do this to me," she asked.

She was angry that he denied her access to go Home. I asked her if she had any messages for anyone, and she said no and that I needed to help her right now before she was, again, denied access. She was in a huge hurry. She had a powerful personality but still needed help to be released.

This was such a tremendous learning opportunity for me. I had never realized the living could haunt the dead until that moment.

## Not Worthy

Some of the most heartbreaking and saddest souls I routinely cross over are those who tell me: "I was born in sin and died in sin. How could God love a sinner like me?" The harsh reality is this concept of sin is a human construct. These people are programmed to believe they are not worthy. Often, it starts when they are small children. God/Source and the Divine want each of us to return Home.

I had a client several years ago who called me because her brother had died from an overdose. She felt horrible she could never save him or help him. She said that her guilt and grief were paralyzing. She was having a hard time functioning in day-to-day life. She called me because she felt like he was with her. And he was, along with a few other souls.

During this session with my client, she learned that her brother had been raped for years "in the name of God" as a small child. Her father, who was the pastor at the church, unwittingly handed him over to a pedophile deacon to work on a farm as a form of punishment.

For her, this explained his drug addiction. He spent a life-time trying to numb the pain of being raped over and over by several "men of the cloth." Her family was a devout religious family and of the type of religion that held a punitive God.

## Suicide

I have crossed over countless souls who have died by suicide and it's one of the most tragic forms of death we may experience. There are also several common themes among this type of death.

This form of violence against oneself is of a very low frequency. This form of death resonates outward and encompasses all of that person's loved ones, including family, friends, and co-workers. Suicide also has a lot of stigma and judgment attached to it.

Frequently, we are told that a person who commits suicide will be banished to hell for eternity and that the person who died by suicide deserves this. Nothing could be further from the truth.

A person who commits suicide is a soul that may be haunted by all sorts of dark beings or may be severely depressed and not know how to escape it. This situation worsens because they don't want to share their pain. They don't want to make their loved ones suffer or worry about them, so they hide it and take their own lives. Sometimes, the suffering person is afraid that they will 'contaminate' others or that those around them may think they are crazy for what is happening to them, and they decide to end their lives.

We need to approach suicide victims with love, kindness, and compassion. While they are no longer in a physical body, their soul, their essence, still lives on, and that soul still needs care, love, kindness, and compassion. Perhaps even more important than that, they ALWAYS need help to go Home, to cross over to Heaven. I'll explain why.

When a soul dies by suicide, they seldom, ever cross over. The reason is basic math. Their frequency is so low they cannot see the light that comes for them. When I work on the 'other side' to help these souls cross over, it's dark with an almost fog-like surrounding.

My analogy is this: Imagine yourself in a dense fog bank, and when you put your hand in front of your face, the fog is so thick you cannot see your own face. How could you see the light that is right in front of you? The answer is you don't.

Then, the light begins to fade away, and you are stuck in a dense daze. Lost.

What makes this form of death even more cruel is that the torture they endured in life continues in death. These souls now reside in the $4^{th}$ dimension, where dark entities seek souls to feed off.

This is a heartbreaking thought.

One of the most potent spiritual acts we can perform is to help these souls to cross over. We all have the power within ourselves to do this. These tortured souls need our help. One of the most spiritually profound acts we humans on earth can take is to help a suicide victim to cross over, to go Home, to see the God they were denied here on earth. It will shift the direction of their soul and their soul's evolution for the better in perpetuity.

What happens when a soul who dies by suicide lingers in limbo? Their souls cannot evolve. Dark beings chronically and constantly harass them. Their soul may also latch onto the living because they don't know what to do or where to go. They may also have feelings of regret and remorse for what they put you through.

## Is It Possible That Suicide Is Contagious?

One of the most remarkable calls I have ever received was from a young woman who lives on another continent. Somehow, she found me and called. She told me that she had been having suicidal thoughts for a long time and that they were getting stronger and stronger. She didn't want to kill herself, and she didn't know why she was feeling this way.

She also told me she was close to getting fired at work and has had many undiagnosed health issues over the past year. As she was talking, I could see them. All of them. There seemed to be more than a dozen of them.

That's when I asked her, "Who do you know that has committed suicide?"

"I have 17 family members who have killed themselves. There are grandparents, aunts, uncles, cousins, and a brother. It seems to be our family curse," she said.

I went on to tell her that all these family members were hanging on her and that she, by no fault of her own, was in resonance with suicide. We immediately worked together and crossed them all over during that same phone call. I explained that her relatives weren't haunting her to be vicious or cruel. They didn't know where to go or what to do.

As each person had committed suicide, they all glommed onto a particular family member. Then, that living family member also committed suicide because they were in resonance with those suicidal family members.

When the dead haunt the living, they can embed their soul energy or frequency into us. When this happens, it makes it hard to distinguish what is our grief and what is the grief of the suicidal soul. This is especially difficult when we don't know that our deceased loved one is with us. We 'just feel bad' or not like ourselves.

I hope that by crossing all of her suicided family members over, we changed her family pattern. I suspect this particular family group kept reincarnating from the 4$^{th}$ dimension over and over, not because they 'deserved' it or were 'bad' people. Still, they didn't know how to cross over or, even if that was possible. It's a great example of how karma doesn't waste energy. This woman had the courage to reach out to a stranger for help.

As an epilogue, she called me a couple of months later to report that her health issues were gone, she had gotten a promotion, and she was engaged to be married. She had her life back and was so grateful.

This situation has made me think about teen suicide and the possible reasons for its massive increase over the past decade. If we can spread the knowledge and power to help these souls upon death, could we then significantly reduce suicide? It's an excellent question to ask ourselves.

Those are just a few reasons why a soul may not cross over. We need to realize that once we leave our physical body, our karmic time here is done for now. Not forever, but for now.

As tragic as those above reasons are, there is also one major, chillingly key reason why a soul may be unable to cross over. The dark beings who descended from the Lucifer Rebellion -- also known as demons or demonic entities-- need a food source because they don't have access to the light energy of the Divine, the Heavens. Those beings became desperate, clever, and cunning.

Perhaps it's our job to help souls cross over, and when we do, we perform a tremendous service to humanity that can change the path of our collective souls for many millennia.

# THE REINCARNATION CYCLE
# IS NOT WHAT IT SEEMS

T he concept of reincarnation has existed throughout the history of this planet. It's found in many of our holy texts, and the idea has been stricken from several sacred texts. Why would our 'spiritual leaders' remove the concept of reincarnation? The jury is still out on the real reasons, but it could be a power play based on greed and, quite possibly, those dark entities puppeteering the living.

Think about it. Traditionally, the teaching has been if you have only one lifetime to live, you need to get it right to head over to those Pearly Gates. You have to follow the rules, right? Who's rules? After all, eternal hell and damnation don't sound that great. Your belief system is based on fear and control. You listen to those in charge. You obey their commands and teachings. You never stray. If we think about our souls and our soul evolution, why would our Creator give us only one shot? Only one mortal life? There is so much to learn that one lifetime is not enough.

The following may sound a bit blasphemous, but here goes . . . We blindly assume that all babies born come from Heaven. Let me repeat this: We blindly assume that all babies born come from Heaven. What if this was not the case? What if the dark entities in the fourth dimension also have control of the reincarnation cycle? What if they reincarnate all those trapped ghostly souls whenever they choose? Guess what? They do.

In this work that I have been doing, I have dealt with some of the worst black magicians and learned a lot from them. I have learned that when they can trap a ghost and prevent it from crossing over, they have access and control over that soul's reincarnation cycle. "They" those dark entities can determine when, where, and how a soul comes back to a mortal body. When this happens, that soul never receives soul restoration, healing, or guidance from the Heavens. They return more broken and corrupted each time.

Are serial killers Heaven sent? What about pedophiles? Would a returning soul who had the proper care, healing, and soul restoration be so inclined to create horrors? Or would they have the strength to resist and perhaps make more positive choices? These are good questions worth pondering.

A soul who does not cross over should never be assumed to be a person who lived an evil or immoral life. Is it possible that this former mortal human is simply a POW? A prisoner of war existing in another dimension. A dimension where time doesn't exist.

All souls need to cross over, and it's not ours to judge where they go. This is above our pay grade, meaning it is not for us to decide who is worthy and who is not. Understanding this concept is essential, and it carries with it a lot of karma.

We, as mortals, have been conditioned or programmed to judge if a person 'is worthy' of crossing over, going Home, or going to Heaven. All souls need to return Home. There is a saying that in my house, there are many mansions. If we look at these mansions on a frequency scale, then these "mansions" represent a certain level of spiritual attainment. A person who has had many incarnations with a spiritual mission of improving humanity will have a higher vibration than that of a serial pedophile. If you do the math, we can understand that these two souls may not end up in the same mansion.

As a public school teacher, I have met several kids whose behavior I questioned. They tended towards violence and, in general, lacked compassion and kindness. Do children who come straight from Heaven, GodSource, have such anomalies? This isn't a judgment call. It's just an observation to ponder. The reality is, I don't know.

I learned a lot about the dark side, the fourth dimension, and all sorts of beings and entities that do not have a physical body. Had I not been thrown into the turbulent paranormal pool without a life vest and struggled to survive, I would not have gained the skills, insights, and wisdom I use today.

My teaching career afforded me many opportunities that helped me on my journey. I valued my time in the classroom and loved teaching children. I learned much about humanity. I have applied the skills I learned in school to many aspects of my life. My first teaching career gave me the skills necessary so I could educate the masses with my second teaching career. That is what I do today.

I learned that there is no healing without God. I also learned that love transcends dimensions. It has to be because love is a form of energy. I also learned that all souls, no matter how they lived or died, need to go Home to cross over into the Heaven World.

Initially, I spent much time figuring out what to do with ghosts. Every ghost I encountered taught me something I would carry within my soul for an eternity. I learned that life as a ghost is not filled with comfort and love. Life as a ghost is a cold and grey place. A ghost is chronically hungry. Ghosts often have to deal with dark entities trying to escape their grasp.

In addition to figuring out the ghost issue my family was dealing with, I also spent a lot of time getting my you-know-what kicked by countless dark entities who were not impressed with my ability to cross over ghostly souls- their food supply.

When we cross over the dead, send them Home. Only then is that soul afforded the opportunities of healing, soul restoration, and guidance of the mortal life just lived with the help of Divine beings. This never will happen in the 4$^{th}$ dimension.

*What if we, as a collective, can clean up the 4$^{th}$ dimension by simply crossing over all the dead stuck there?* Those dark entities are now denied an energy source they have had access to for a long time.

I have had the privilege of crossing over some of the world's worst pedophiles and murderers. I consider it a privilege because those dark souls can no longer influence the living mortals. They cannot influence other mortals to become a pedophile. They cannot expand their dark empire because now they are in the hands of God, Source, or the Divine. They can no longer impact the living. The 4$^{th}$ dimension significantly impacts our 3$^{rd}$ dimension, and it's time we take our power back to live the lives we were meant to live.

I had a client who was repeatedly raped by a neighbor as a young girl. She grew up with a single mom who kept sending her back to the rapist so he could babysit her while the mom was trying to earn a living. Life has not been easy for this client, yet she is a good person.

Here is where it got interesting. She called me because her childhood rapist had died. No one told her he had died. Yet, she knew he was dead. How did she know this? His ghost showed up at her home, and he tried to rape her as a ghost. Yes, it can happen. We crossed him over together so that he could not influence the living.

When she crossed her rapist over and sent him to the Heaven World, she regained her personal power. A piece of her soul was stolen from her at a young age. She was finally *free*. He could no longer harass or harm her because she had the wisdom and insight to do something that seemed counterintuitive- sending her rapist Home to Heaven.

## Spiritual Tools

Who can cross over the dead? We all can. You don't need a psychic, minister, priest, shaman, or any other person to do this service. The first ingredient you need is the compassion in your heart and the ability to know you are working for the greater good, no matter how a soul lived or died. It's that simple.

The next ingredient to crossing over ghosts is angels. I am sharing with you what I know to be true and what works because you can build upon this knowledge in your own right. Having dealt with countless black magicians, I have learned one of the easiest ways to free a soul trapped in the 4th dimension is by using the power of angels.

It goes back to frequency. Angels are spiritual beings with a high frequency. Dark entities are spiritual beings with a low frequency. They hang onto ghosts to control, manipulate, and drain them of their light source and negatively influence the living. When you request an angel to cross over a loved one, that angel's presence is so high, and their blinding light is so bright that they cannot hold onto those ghosts.

It's not much different than touching a hot stove. We get burnt and let go. Those dark ones cannot hold onto a ghost when angels arrive on the scene. Those angels will then, in turn, take that soul Home.

Remember that angels are here to assist us with our mortal journey. They are here to serve us and love us unconditionally. Because we have free will and can make choices and decisions, we need to remember they require us to request their help. This is what got Lucifer's panties all in a bunch- he didn't have free will and, became angry at God and left Heaven.

This is why it's essential as we request angelic help to be specific in our appeals. There are many types of angels, and when it comes to crossing over the dead, there are angels who help with just that. They assist lost souls so that they may go Home. Prayers that come from the heart are extremely powerful. Often, it can be as simple as "I am requesting Angels from the higher realms to come and cross over *insert name* to the higher realms right now."

Sometimes, when a loved one dies, it can be difficult to cross over that loved one. Our grief can be so intense that it may make it impossible to cross them over.

If you find that you tend to be a 'ghost magnet,' you can request angels from the higher realms to help you to cross over ghosts.

I am often asked what it feels like to cross over someone. What should that person expect? The answer is varied. It depends upon the soul's energy that was crossed over and that of the living person and their level of sensitivity. People often comment that they felt some unexplained energy shift or feel lighter. Sometimes, they tell me that things all of a sudden look brighter to them.

There is no one correct answer. It just comes from within the heart.

## More Than Angels

Building your frequency is also important, as it helps keep you in a safer space. As we know by now, it's not just ghosts that reside in the 4th dimension.

We have all heard the saying, "Cleanliness is next to Godliness." It's not just a saying that we appreciate as small children or teenagers; there's a rationale for this mantra: Being clean raises our frequency.

When our belongings are cleaned and organized, we think clearer and tend not to lose our keys or phones. There is order and less chaos. It can also reduce our anxieties. But let's be honest, it's not always easy. We lead full lives, and we get busy. It's important to realize we can clean our spaces on multiple levels.

The following tools and ideas help you clean and clear your personal spaces as you consciously improve your spiritual path.

## Salt

Let's take a look at the concept of salt. Salt cleanses. Go to the ocean and breathe in the salty air, and you start to feel better. We used to use salt to preserve our meat before refrigeration. Salt kept bacteria and decomposition at bay. It kept the meat safe to eat. Salt will also (painfully so) clean wounds. But it works.

Another way to use salt in your spiritual practices is through visualization. You can use it to clear and clean your spaces. In a quiet room, sit or lie down and close your eyes. Visualize yourself pouring down a rain of salt in your home. You can do it room by room, from the top down, or however best it works for you. With practice, you will become more proficient at it. Just remember, salt cleanses in all dimensions.

## The Importance of Violet Flame

This is another form of visualization. Learning to use this powerful tool of light energy is spiritually cleansing. It helps to remove negative energies within or surrounding us. It transmutes that negative energy, which is critical to making the world a better place. When you transmute that negative energy, you are not polluting the ether.

Look at it this way: if you drive in your car and stop for iced tea on a road trip, what do you do with the paper cup and straw? Do you properly dispose of them, or do you roll down your window and toss them out the door?

Do you remember as a child learning the acronym Roy G. BIV? Each letter represents a color of the rainbow, in order of the frequency and light wavelengths of that light spectrum- red, orange, yellow, green, blue, indigo, and VIOLET. Violet is the highest frequency of the visual light spectrum.

Go online and look at a visual representation of a violet flame. This is the most straightforward way to learn how to visualize it. Once you have done that, go to a quiet place and practice bringing up a violet flame. You can visualize yourself being surrounded by it or your home, car, or office space. It may seem difficult initially, but the more you practice, the easier and quicker it becomes.

These tools are called spiritual practices for a reason-- we need to practice!

When I clear my spaces or those of a client, I often combine salt and violet flame. I will visualize a violet flame coming up from the ground below while at the same time bringing down a rain salt. They work wonderfully together.

# REMOVING THE AIRY FAIRY
# AND PIXIE DUST

There are a lot of false spiritual tools that don't work, and they let the dark side sneak in without much notice. The first element that needs to be addressed is something called spiritual bypassing.

Spiritual bypassing happens when we use spiritual concepts to sidestep authentic healing, creating a false sense of enlightenment. We compromise our souls when we use spiritual practices to compensate for true soul healing and restoration.

Utilizing spiritual practices and teachings to cover up our issues, such as low self-esteem, financial ramifications, constant and chronic relationship problems, and not dealing with fears, are some signs of spiritual bypassing. Our egos play a large part in spiritual bypassing.

Spiritual bypassing is also a defense mechanism that creates a false sense of truth so we don't deal with our problems, and then we can blame others for how we conduct our lives.

## Sage

Remember the sage story in Section 11? I learned a lot about frequency from that experience. Sage is a wonderful medicinal herb. It's quite beneficial but never meant to clear a space of ghosts or other dark entities. How is it that this herb was maligned so much? Why did that happen? Could it be that the dark side, those demonic beings in the 4th dimension, imparted this knowledge to keep us suffering in the hopes of keeping us from seeking fundamental knowledge and power? Sage doesn't have the spiritual horsepower to remove ghosts or dark entities. And if it did, where would sage send them?

Looking back through history, this question arises: Why was the Christ child gifted frankincense, gold, and myrrh? Why didn't those wise men give the Christ child sage? The reason is frequency. All three of those gifts vibrate at a high frequency, and the Christ child needed all the support he could get while living in a mortal body.

It's worth rethinking the role of sage in our lives. Sage is a vital herb with many uses, but we should be reasonable about our expectations of it.

## Divination Cards

There are hundreds of types of divination cards out there. Tarot cards were initially created by European artists who were commissioned by the nobility or the wealthy and were considered simple parlor games and not as divinatory tools. It wasn't until around the 18th century that the purpose of these cards changed as people started to assign meanings to each card.

It was then that the occult began to find these cards of interest.

Angel cards, tarot cards, and runes are just a few of these cards on the market today. There are tarot decks for any profession or hobby, from The Lord of the Rings to baseball and zombies. These divination cards are littered all over the earth.

They come in many forms, and many have pretty pictures on them. They look so unassuming, benign, and downright harmless. Pick a card, lay out a spread, and you will get information from 'the other side.' But what 'other side' is feeding you the information? How do you really know? How do you know if you are being led by ego and that is compromising you?

Sounds pretty good? Sounds simple? Sounds easy? Perhaps a bit too good to be true? The issue with these cards is that it's tough to understand where the information comes from. We want to assume it's coming from someone on our spiritual team, one of the good guys. But how do we know if the information comes from our spiritual team or a shape-shifter excited to wreak some havoc?

You could have inadvertently permitted these dark entities to attach to you. They will also expect some form of payment extraction. Nothing in life is free because karma always seeks balance. If there is anything we can learn from these cards and other tools, we have the power within ourselves to have a straight connection to GodSource.

We don't need to depend upon contrived devices.

I remember a client that I had who was a tarot reader. She had come to me because she felt she kept having financial blocks. As we were working together on her issue, I saw that she had a LOT of dark entities with her. As we were rounding them up, one of the dark entities offered this bit of information: Tarot cards can become easily corrupted, and the dark side uses them to make portals so that they have easier access to living mortals. The dark side loves these cards in all their forms.

A friend had given my number to her cousin because she was looking for help. She had suffered an unimaginable loss, and she wanted to know if God was punishing her for something she had done in her past. As a child, her family had attended one of those churches where 'you are born in sin and will die in sin' and that God was vengeful and full of wrath.

I asked her what she had done that was so sinful. She explained that she and some friends had gone out drinking a few times as a teenager. I wondered if there was anyone out there who didn't do something dumb as a teenager. I assured her God wouldn't punish her for this and asked her what her issue was. What was she seeking to resolve?

She told me that she and her husband lost their baby boy to SIDS around four months of age, about a year prior. She and her husband had difficulties, which is expected under these circumstances. She also mentioned they had been try-ing to conceive with no luck. They even went to the doctor to see if something was wrong. They were both in perfect health. She thought that the death of their child and the inability to conceive another child was God's way of punishing her.

I then picked up on something. My intuition told me to ask her if she had tarot cards in the house. At first, she said no. I kept telling her I was picking up on this tarot card vibe and to look around.

She called me back about an hour later and told me she found a deck. She had forgotten that her aunt had given her this deck years ago as a birthday present. She had opened the box of cards at one point and didn't know what to do with them, so she had tucked them away in her underwear drawer and forgot about them.

I told her that we should do an experiment. She ripped each card in half, put a piece of aluminum foil at the bottom of her grill, and burned each card. She said it took a long time, and when she finished, she wrapped all the ashes in the foil and tossed them. The next day, she thanked me and said she felt much better.

Six weeks later, she called to tell me that she was pregnant. They now have three adorable little girls and a happy family life.

## Spells

Spells are another form of divination that can get us into trouble on our spiritual path. In the section on the 3rd dimension, the concept of free will was discussed. Living mortals have the free will to make decisions. Every decision we make earns us karma. We need to remember that karma is not emotional, not judgmental, or punishing. Karma seeks balance.

A spell is designed to take away someone else's free will. What type of karma is earned when one living mortal takes away the free will of another? Do you really want to cast a spell on someone to make them love you? Or cast a spell against someone so that they suffer?

Spells fuel dark entities, and it's possible that you could sell your soul to the dark side with this activity.

## Ouija Boards

What's the harm in a game made by a world-famous toy company? It's known as a 'spirit board' where the living can contact 'spirits.' The issue becomes what kind of spirits are being contacted.

Beings from the light side, or Heavens, would never use a board like this to communicate with the living, as it would violate spiritual law. They are bound by constructs when it comes to interfering with our free will. They are not allowed to interfere in this manner. This leads to the question: What types of beings actually come through when using this board?

The shapeshifter pretending to be a grandma is a very common and dangerous scenario.

What do you do if you have one of these boards? Whatever you do, do not donate it or give it to someone. You are karmically responsible for that action and what may happen to another person. If at all possible, rip the board and break the pieces up. If you can safely burn it, then do so. If not, wrap it up in aluminum foil (shiny side in) and dispose of it.

You can also do the same with any spell books or divination cards.

These instruments keep the dark side active and fed energetically. These tools actually take away our inner power to connect to high-level beings. We need to understand that each of us can have a direct connection to God, and we do not need these tools to do this for us. We don't need an intermediary. We don't even need buildings made of wood and stone to connect to God or Source. It takes patience, intention, and practice through prayer and meditation. When we pray, we are talking to GodSource. When we meditate, we are listening.

Remember, you are worth it. You can set aside time each day for prayer and meditation, even if it's only a few minutes. It's also your right to set aside time each day to study and read. It's essential to start and set a pattern or schedule for yourself. No one can do this for you. Only you can.

This is an essential aspect of our spiritual paths; karma will reward us for taking the time to do this. A good time to pray and meditate is before you go to sleep and when you wake up. I like the calm, quiet energy of those times of the day. This is just my preference, and it works for me.

Books on healing, spirituality, and metaphysics are some of my favorites. I tend to read several books simultaneously, mostly because I grab the book I need to read. I have some standard books that I read over and over. Discover what works for you. You deserve it.

## Intuition

Intuition is critical when we embark on our spiritual path. In fact, intuition is our most potent and profound psychic ability. Unfortunately, many of us have been denied the ability to listen to our intuition and trust our gut feeling at an early age. We get denied by those in charge when we think we know something or when we intrinsically know how to do something.

Children who are allowed to develop their intuition naturally will, in general, behave in a manner that is calm and less reactionary. When we learn to develop and rely on our intuition, we start to listen on a deeper level. This gives us wisdom and insight. The ability to listen also gives us access to the Divine, to the beings in the Heavens.

How can we build our intuition? One way is to journal. Write down a question to which you want to know the answer, then set down the journal, return to that question later on, and free-write. You may surprise yourself.

Pay attention to your dreams. Our dreams are often symbolic of messages that we need to hear. They may appear in metaphor form, which can be frustrating, but look at the metaphors as a puzzle that needs solving.

Doing something that is creative and that you enjoy will open you up to intuitive thoughts and emotions. The same is true for exercise such as running or swimming. When we do these activities, we tend to 'get in the zone.'

Pay attention to your sudden feelings or your gut instinct on a situation or a person. Take a moment and ask yourself why you are feeling this way. What is this feeling telling me? What do I need to know? What is your body's reaction? Is it visceral? Is it exciting?

Sometimes, doing repetitive activities such as washing dishes or doing yard work will give your mind the quiet it needs to solve a problem. Don't fight your intuitive thoughts.

This may not be easy at first, especially if you were programmed as a child not to trust yourself. Make it a challenge when you come up with a situation. Take a moment to be in the moment. Absorb that feeling, explore it, and then pause and act or react to the problem being presented to you.

Look at it as a karmic quiz. Did you pass?

Most importantly, know that when you practice relying on your intuition, it gives you a more profound knowledge, and it's a powerful force that will provide you with wisdom and an edge in life. Don't deny yourself this fundamental ability to own your power. Intuition should be looked at as a discovery process to enhance your life. Throughout my trials and tribulations trying to figure out the unseen world, I never valued and trusted my intuition more.

The world has been in a spiritual crisis for a long time. What would happen if we all learned to develop our intuition for the greater good? How would the world benefit?

I want to leave you with three thoughts, or rather secrets. They are rather simple yet poignant.

**Secret #1:**
The key is simple. Spiritual teams are karmically earned. We all have spiritual teams. When we learn to ask for angelic help, seek out the greater good, and develop our intuition, we raise our frequency and enhance our karmic paths. Enhance our soul's evolution.

**Secret # 2:**
Remember the Star Trek series? They always seemed to be talking about the ships' shields. "Shields are holding at 80%." "Shields are down to 20%, and we can't hold on much longer."

What the crew in these Sci-Fi television shows and movies are talking about is how well they are protected. Learn what you can do to help protect yourself so you can be proactive and live a smoother life with wisdom and spiritual insights. Karma always wants to know if you learned the lessons. Learning psychic self-defense is common sense. It helps to keep us safe from the unseen world.

This is not meant to instill fear but to help us understand that we can and do have the power to make changes within ourselves.

**Secret #3:**

The phrase, "In my house, there are many mansions," is an important one to understand. It's not ours to judge what happens to a soul upon death. What we do need to understand is that no matter how a soul lived or died, every single soul needs to go Home.

Only when we can achieve this will we oust the dark entities that keep invading our beautiful planet. These dark ones rely on our ignorance, which gives them the upper hand. When we cross over a soul who has committed dark deeds, we give them to the light side. The Heavens and those higher-dimensional beings now have access to that soul for healing, restoration, and counselors to help them understand the life (or lives) they lived.

When a soul is trapped between dimensions, it will often reincarnate from the 4th dimension and come back here already in a spiritual crisis. It's not ours to judge where a soul should go upon death. That is the job of the higher realm beings. How many times have we heard someone hoping that a person who dies 'goes to hell'?

There is so much more to the human experience than we know exists. Possibilities and potentials are limitless. The rise in technologies helps to validate the unseen world. I sincerely hope the information in this book is helpful and informative. I intimately know what loneliness, doubts, and the questioning of one's sanity is like. I know I am not unique in these experiences. If this book and my experiences can help even one person to navigate through these tumultuous paranormal waters with a more profound sense of wisdom, insight, and strength, it will have been worth it.

After a tough night battling the dark side, my daughter came in, hugged me, and handed me this note. This is what drives me to this day.

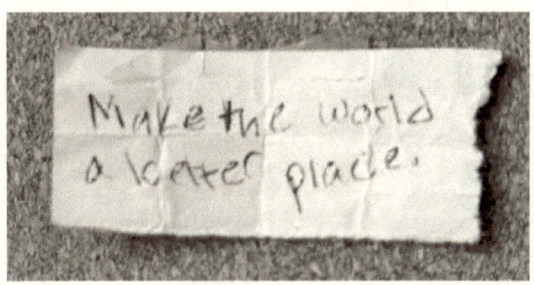

*Love, Laura*

# ACKNOWLEDGMENTS

To CS, who could be my CS Lewis, because you have such great words. ☺ Thank you for being by my side, unconditionally there for me in all ways. I love you and your family, whom I consider my family.

Susie Schaefer, Joe Estrada and, Amit Dey. Thank you for your efforts and dedication to make this book the best possible. I appreciate your time, dedication, and love for this project.

# ABOUT THE AUTHOR

 A Remote Viewer, Author, and Speaker, Laura Van Tyne holds a B.S. in Education, a B.A. in Spanish, and a Master's degree in Second Language Acquisition, with much of her life spent as a middle school teacher.

Twenty years ago, the paranormal realm broke through her home, and she stopped teaching to determine how to keep her family safe. Today, she helps others with similar problems when faced with the unseen world.

Laura focuses on soul health and how we can create a healthy soul. The unseen, energetic world impacts soul health and mitigates our free will. When we learn to discern other-worldly beings - who they indeed are and where they come from, we take our power back. And when we learn to connect with the light beings, we can attain wisdom, insight, and fantastic assistance along our karmic journey.

Reincarnation is a part of our soul experiences. We all die; however, we rarely discuss what to do upon death. That is the key to soul health, wellness, and sovereignty. Laura specializes in Past Life Regression, Etheric Implant Removal, Quantum Healing Hypnosis, MILAB Abduction, Soul Integration, and Spiritual Self-Defense.

For more information about how to work with Laura, online programs, speaking engagements, and additional services, visit thekarmicpath.com